with my best wishes

Philip Whitehead

TITANIC

"WAITING FOR ORDERS"

THE STORY OF ALEXANDER JAMES LITTLEJOHN
STEWARD TO W. T. STEAD

BEFORE THE DISASTER

AFTER THE DISASTER

*"All the men in our department stood at the boats
and not one of us moved until ordered into the boats."*

Alexander Littlejohn, First Class Steward, The *Titanic*

First published April 1999

ISBN 0 9535436 0 9

Published by:
The Crescent Company
PO Box 348
Maidenhead
SL6 6XB
UK

Designed by - Jason Horsburgh
Printed by - Gemini Press Ltd

CONTENTS

Alexander James Littlejohn

1. EARLY YEARS

Alexander, Clement & Emily 1876

Alexander & Clement 1883

My grandfather, Alexander James Littlejohn was born on the 6th March 1872 at 1 Globe Street, St George in the East, London.

His parents, Alexander and Emily Littlejohn, maintained the tradition of the first born son being given the family name Alexander. This can be traced back to an Alexander Littlejohn, born 1755, in Aberdeen, Scotland. Alexander James' father had followed the family trade of miller's and bakers, working as a miller's traveller and his grandfather and great-grandfather as master baker's. Alexander had an sister Emily (born 1869) and a brother Clement (born 1875).

The young Alexander was not to follow the family traditions. As a boy he went to sea and sailed in many types of ship although he gave this up in 1898 to become the licensee of *The Rising Sun* public house, Hammond Street, Cheshunt, Hertfordshire. (Sadly, one hundred years later, in 1998, *The Rising Sun* was demolished to make way for a new housing estate.) This change of career may well have been influenced by his uncle, Thomas Littlejohn, who worked as a wine manager.

His mother had died in 1886 and his father, brother and sister all lived in the Cheshunt area. On the 12th June 1899, Alexander married Anne Louisa Gocher, a 23-year-old farmer's daughter from Cheshunt. In 1900 she bore his first son, Alexander Francis (known as Alick), in *The Rising Sun*.

In 1901 he moved to Hastings, East Sussex where he became the landlord of *The Crown Inn*, All Saints Street. This was one of the main coaching inns in Hastings, with extensive stabling for the horse-drawn coaches that brought parties from London to Hastings throughout the Victorian period.

The Crown, still exists, serving the busy fishing community in Hastings Old Town. It is interesting to note that the present landlord, Alexander Napier rings time with a reproduction *Titanic* bell. Alex had not known about his predecessor's connection with the *Titanic*.

In 1902, his second son (my father) Henry Alfred (known as Harry) was born at *The Crown Inn*. Anne suffered from poor health and after a daughter Winifred May was born in 1907 she never fully recovered. Alexander became ill with rheumatism which affected his sight and in 1909 gave up *The Crown* to return to Cheshunt. It was here, on the 28th February 1910, that Anne died at the age of 34 years, and was buried in Cheshunt Cemetery.

He decided to return to sea, sending Harry to his Uncle Clement and Aunt Emily, in Manor Park, London, Winifred to a Miss Chance, at Park House, Hammond Street, Cheshunt, and Alick to The Royal Masonic School, Bushey, Hertfordshire.

Above: Anne Gocher, who Alexander married in 1899, and who died in 1910. Right: Alexander & Anne (left) at The Rising Sun 1899.

Above: Alexander (left) with Emily & Clement (seated) at The Rising Sun. Top Centre: The Rising Sun, Hammond Street, Cheshunt, 1898 Below: Alexander's Birth Certificate.

Book, No. 26	Page 57	Certificate of Birth.						
1872	Birth in the Sub-District of *Saint John*			in the County of *Middlesex*				
No.	When and where Born.	Name (if any).	Sex.	Name and Surname of Father.	Name and Maiden Surname of Mother.	Rank or Profession of Father.	Signature, Description, and Residence of Informant.	When Registered.	Signature of Registrar.	Baptismal Name, if added after Registration of Birth.
284	Sixth March 1872. 1 Globe Street.	Alexander James	Boy	Alexander Littlejohn	Emily Matilda Littlejohn formerly Giles.	Miller's Traveller	Emily Matilda Littlejohn mother 1 Globe Street St George in the East	Sixteenth April 1872.	Alexander Littlejohn Registrar.	

I Certify that the above is a true Copy of an Entry in the Register Book of Births in the Registrar's District of *Saint John* in the Superintendent Registrar's District of *Saint George in the East* in the County of *London* And I further Certify that the said Register Book is lawfully in my custody. Witness my hand this *Third* day of *August* 1893.

Harry T. Dudman, Deputy Superintendent Registrar.

Above: Emily & Anne with the boys at Hastings 1905.

Left: View of The Crown Inn, *All Saints Street, Hastings c1902.*

Alexander, Anne & their first child Alexander Francis 1900.

Alexander in his Masonic regalia, Hastings 1904.

Emily with Alexander Francis (standing) & Henry (author's father seated) 1905.

Alexander's sons with his father 1906.

Alexander's first voyage, as a steward, started on the 5th January 1911 when he sailed from Tilbury on the P & O liner the *Orsova* (6,830 tons) bound for Australia. In 1911 the round trip to Australia took three months so he did not return to Tilbury until the 15th April - little did he realise the significance that this date would have in his life exactly one year later.

His experience in the licensed trade must have given him knowledge that would have come in useful as a steward, serving passengers in First Class dining rooms and saloons.

In May 1911 he joined the White Star Line and sailed from Southampton on the 3rd May aboard the *Adriatic* (15,637 tons) bound for New York. He returned to Southampton on the 25th May. He had now obtained lodgings at 11 Western Terrace, Chapel, Southampton (now demolished) where he lived between voyages.

On the 14th June 1912 he joined the new White Star liner the *Olympic* on her maiden voyage to New York. The *Olympic* was commanded by Captain Edward John Smith, aged 61, and nearing the end of a distinguished career with the White Star Line. He planned to make just one more maiden voyage after this - that of the *Olympic's* sister ship, the *Titanic*, which had been launched the previous month in Belfast.

The White Star Line had commissioned Harland & Wolff of Belfast to build a new Olympic Class of ships, of which the *Olympic* (45,324 tons), was the first. She was to be followed by sister ships, the *Titanic*, and the *Gigantic* (later called the *Britannic*). These three ships were to compete with the Cunard liners, the *Mauritania*, and the *Lusitania*, both over 31,000 tons with a top speed of 26 knots, which had been launched in 1907. The White Star decided not to compete on speed, (although the *Olympic* class ships were capable of 24 - 25 knots), but on size, luxury, and safety. *It was never claimed that these ships were 'unsinkable' - only that they were 'practically unsinkable'.*

The maiden voyage of the *Olympic* was a far greater media event than that of the *Titanic* some 11 months later. Newsreels of the time purporting to be of the *Titanic*, were in fact of the maiden voyage of the *Olympic*.

The *Olympic* set new standards in luxury. First Class had, in addition to its luxury cabins and spacious dining room; a large reception room, a huge lounge, a smoking room, reading room, a Verandah Cafe, a grand staircase topped with a glass dome, a swimming pool, Turkish baths, and a gymnasium. Three elevators were installed to take First Class passengers from one deck to another. Another elevator was for use of Second Class passengers. The whole concept of the ship was based on the idea of a First Class hotel, particularly the a' la carte restaurant, which imitated the fashionable *Ritz* restaurants that the ships of the Hamburg-Amerika Line possessed. Hence, many passengers referred to the a' la carte restaurant on the *Olympic* as the *Ritz*.

Even for stewards, the *Olympic* set new standards in accommodation. For the first time stewards had proper bathrooms, but this innovation did not last for long, as these became store rooms and stewards resorted to their traditional bucket for a wash.

Thomas Andrews,
Managing Director
of Harland & Wolff.

Bruce Ismay,
Chairman of the
White Star Line

On leaving Southampton, the *Olympic* sailed across the Channel to Cherbourg to take on further passengers and discharge those few passengers who had used the vessel to make the crossing to France. The *Olympic* was too large to dock at Cherbourg so she was met by the tenders the *Traffic* and the *Nomadic* which had been completed by Harland and Wolff at the same time as the *Olympic* The *Nomadic* survives to this day as a floating restaurant on the Seine in Paris.

The return maiden voyage of the *Olympic*, New York to Southampton ended with discharge for Alexander on the 5th July 1911. He then took part in two further return journeys to New York on the *Olympic* commencing on the 9th and 30th August respectively, shore leave between these voyages being just three days in Southampton. If these voyages were uneventful the next certainly was not.

The *Olympic* sailed from Berth 44/45 Southampton on the 20th September bound for New York. She had just left Southampton Water and entered The Solent when she was in collision with the cruiser H.M.S. *Hawke*. The two ships had been travelling on parallel courses when the *Hawke* was sucked into the side of the *Olympic*. The *Olympic* under the command of Captain E. J. Smith was badly damaged by the ram shaped bow of the cruiser. The passengers had to be taken off and returned to Southampton by tender. That night the *Olympic* lay at anchor off the Isle of Wight waiting for the high tide so she could return to Southampton. Alexander had the presence of mind to pick up a broken piece of porthole glass and put it in his pocket. (It is now part of my collection of memorabilia.) After this early discharge for the crew, and a few days unplanned and unpaid shore leave, Alexander set out once more for New York, this time on the *Majestic* arriving back in Southampton on the 15th October.

Then followed a lengthy period of shore leave while the *Olympic* was undergoing repairs. The *Olympic* had returned slowly to Harland and Wolff's yard in Belfast and was berthed alongside the not yet completed *Titanic*. Shipyard workers were taken off the *Titanic* to speed the repairs to the *Olympic*, which delayed the completion of the *Titanic*, and ultimately her maiden voyage, which had been planned for the 20th March 1912.

It was not until the 29th November, that the *Olympic* was once again ready to set sail from Southampton. It had been over six weeks since Alexander had worked in the First Class Dining Room. Life must have been hard without pay, and without the tips from wealthy passengers, upon which the stewards depended. Many passengers on the cross Atlantic route would request to be seated at a table served by a steward they particularly liked, and in return stewards would get to know the individual passengers requirements. At the end of a crossing passengers could be very generous to a steward who had served them well.

The next voyage, starting on the 20th December, meant that he would spend Christmas and see in the New Year (1912), aboard the *Olympic*. The start of this year saw two more Atlantic crossings on the *Olympic,* discharge from the second being on the 28th February. Once again the *Olympic* had to be taken out of service and return to Belfast for the refitting of her port propeller, having dropped a blade on the 24th February while returning from New York.

From the 1st - 6th March, the two liners, the *Olympic* and the *Titanic,* were together for what was to be the last time.

After this enforced time ashore, Alexander travelled to Belfast to join other senior crew and officers on the new liner the *Titanic.* It was from Belfast that Alexander sent a postcard showing the *Titanic* nearing completion docked in the largest graving dock in the world. The postcard (dated March 29th) was sent to his oldest son, Alick, then aged 12, and attending The Royal Masonic School, carrying the following message:

Dear Alick,

Uncle Clem will meet you at Broad Street. The ship goes for her speed trials on Monday and leaves here for Southampton on Tuesday. I hope you will get on allright.(sic.)
from Dad

The speed trials were scheduled to start on the 1st April but strong winds prevented the tugs taking the *Titanic* from the dock basin out into Belfast Lough. Just before 6am on Tuesday 2nd April, the *Titanic* was moved out of the River Lagan into the Victoria Channel leading into Belfast Lough. Here for the first time the *Titanic* moved under her own power. Black smoke poured from her front three funnels, the fourth funnel was for ventilation purposes only. Stokers worked to fire boilers which would provide the steam to drive the *Titanic's* turbines. Lunch was served for the first time on the great ship, not to passengers, but to those crew who could be spared from duty and to representatives of Harland and Wolff and the White Star Line.

Officers of the Olympic *including Captain E. J. Smith (far right), James Moody (second right), William Murdoch (left).*

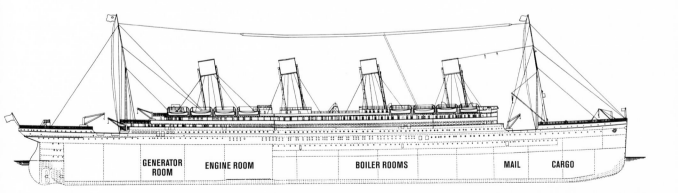

| GENERATOR ROOM | ENGINE ROOM | BOILER ROOMS | MAIL | CARGO |

This was the first meal* that Alexander served aboard the *Titanic*:

Alexander, Australia,
where he travelled on
the Orsova *1911.*

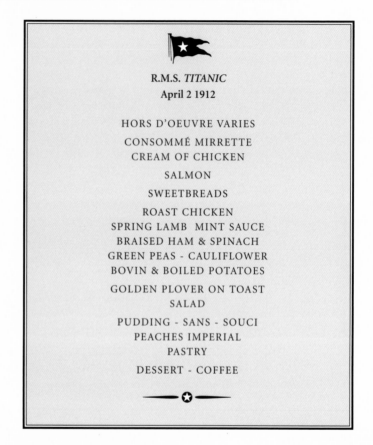

R.M.S. *TITANIC*
April 2 1912

HORS D'OEUVRE VARIES
CONSOMMÉ MIRRETTE
CREAM OF CHICKEN

SALMON

SWEETBREADS

ROAST CHICKEN
SPRING LAMB MINT SAUCE
BRAISED HAM & SPINACH
GREEN PEAS - CAULIFLOWER
BOVIN & BOILED POTATOES

GOLDEN PLOVER ON TOAST
SALAD
PUDDING - SANS - SOUCI
PEACHES IMPERIAL
PASTRY
DESSERT - COFFEE

The authenticity of this menu and the
following morning's breakfast menu, has
been questioned by some researchers.

After lunch the ship carried out an 'emergency stop' test. This involved sailing at full speed towards a marker buoy and having reached it, putting the engines to full astern. From a speed of 20 knots the *Titanic* took 850 yards (773 metres) to come to a halt. The trials were completed by 7pm and the papers were signed to hand the *Titanic* over from her builders to her new owners. The papers were signed for Harland and Wolff by Thomas Andrews, managing director and head of the design department, who, due to the illness of Lord Pirrie, the ship's designer, was to travel on the ship's maiden voyage to New York. The *Titanic* had cost £1,500,000 to build and equip and was the largest movable object made by man.

Just after 8pm on the 2nd April the *Titanic* left Belfast for the final time. The ship had to reach Southampton on the midnight tide the following day. On board the *Titanic* were the two Marconi operators Jack Phillips and Harold Bride testing out their new equipment. They made contact with other ships using the code sign 'MGY' allotted to the *Titanic*. Due to freak weather conditions, they were able to establish contact with Tenerife and Port Said, more than 3,000 miles away.

Alexander served a substantial breakfast to those on board the *Titanic* on the morning of 3rd April. The Edwardian traveller would have expected this degree of choice on such a prestigious ship, but it is doubtful that First Class ladies would have eaten many of these dishes.

R.M.S. *TITANIC*

April 3 1912

FRUIT

QUAKER OATS

FILLETS OF WHITING
KIPPERED HERRINGS
CALVES LIVER & BACON
GRILLED HAM - GRILLED SAUSAGE
MINCED CHICKEN
POACHED & FRIED EGGS
PLAIN & TOMATO OMELETTES
MASHED & SAUTÉ POTATOES

COLD MEAT

ROLLS - SCONES

MARMALADE
STRAWBERRY CONSERVE

WATERCRESS

The card sent by Alexander from Belfast before he set out for Southampton on the Titanic.

2. THE *TITANIC* -
ALEXANDER'S THIRTEENTH VOYAGE

It was just after midnight on the 3rd April, when the tugs finally manoeuvred the liner into Berth 44, White Star Dock (later Ocean Dock) in Southampton.

Since January 1912, Britain had been in the grip of a coal strike and this had resulted in many liners being laid up in Southampton. Those liners still sailing had agreed to a speed restriction of 20 knots. The problem had become so acute that ships were tied up in tandem. Just downstream from the *Titanic* lay the *Oceanic* (inboard) and the *New York* (outboard). The *Titanic* had to be fuelled with coal taken from other ships if her maiden voyage was to commence on the 10th April as planned. There was another problem regarding coal that Captain Smith and his Chief Engineer Bell were aware of. Since leaving Belfast a fire had been smouldering in Number 10 bunker of Number 6 Boiler Room. Despite efforts to extinguish it, the fire was not put out until Easter Sunday.

All crew had to sign on, bringing with them their seamen's log books (the *Certificate of Continuous Discharge*). On Good Friday, the 5th April, the *Titanic* was covered in flags and bunting. All work stopped on Easter Sunday, but on the 8th and 9th April the ship was a hive of activity. Supplies were bought by train onto the keyside and transferred to the ship. Large items of passengers freight, such as the new 1912 model, 25 horsepower Renault car being taken to America by Mr William Carter, were loaded aboard by the dockside cranes and stored in the hold.

The morning of the 10th April saw the passengers begin to arrive. The boat train from Waterloo, carrying Second and Third Class passengers, arrived on the dockside at just before 9.30am. Second Class tickets had cost £13 for an adult. They boarded on 'C' Deck as did those who had bought Third Class or Steerage passenger tickets. Each class had its own entrance and once aboard the classes were segregated from each other by locked wire screen barriers and doors. Many of the passengers in the Third Class were non-English speakers and the maze of corridors and signs must have been very confusing for them. Stewards did their best to help people find their cabins. Third Class cabins were on four of the *Titanic's* decks (D, E, F, and G). Despite having to share with up to five other people in a cabin, the *Titanic* was a great advance on the dormitory type accommodation that was normally given to Third Class passengers. Nowhere on the *Titanic* was any cabin to be found with the number 13, owing to the superstitious nature of seamen.

Many passengers boarding the ship had originally booked onto other liners now taken out of service due to the coal strike. For many this up-grade to the new liner renowned for new standards of luxury would have been a cause for celebration. Despite this the *Titanic* would make her maiden voyage with only two-thirds of her passenger capacity occupied.

At 11.30am the boat train carrying the First Class passengers arrived on the dockside. There were many reporters and photographers ready to record the event as the rich and famous members of society made ready to board the new liner.

Among those interviewed was W. T. Stead, the famous journalist, social reformer and spiritualist, who told them that he had not intended to make the trip, but President Taft had asked him to speak at the World Peace Conference at Carnegie Hall, New York. Alexander would be steward to W. T. Stead during the voyage to New York. By a strange twist of fate W. T. Stead had been close friends with a relative of Alexander's, Matilda Littlejohn who shared his interest in spiritualism.

A newspaper of 1912 described Stead as follows;

"Among the English passengers there was no more brilliant personality than Mr W. T. Stead, undoubtedly the greatest journalist of the age. A man of the keenest and most penetrating intellect when dealing with many subjects of life, a man of large enthusiasms, of high ideals, of restless energy, and with a great gift for laughter, he was a shining light in any kind of company, and made innumerable friends in all ranks of society and in all countries."

William Thomas Stead was a newspaper editor who first came to fame as editor of the London evening paper the *Pall Mall Gazette* In 1890 he started a magazine called the *Review of Reviews* which was a forerunner of todays *Readers Digest*.

A great believer in equal rights for women, he was the first to employ a woman journalist. He worked with General Bramwell Booth, of the Salvation Army, to expose the 'white slave trade' in London where young girls could be 'bought' for prostitution. Booth and Stead planned to expose this trade but their plan went wrong when they staged the 'buying' of a girl of 13, for £5. Stead was tried and given three months in Holloway prison. The resulting publicity helped bring Stead's cause to public notice, including that of the author George Bernard Shaw. The girl in the plan was Liza Armstrong and Shaw used her as the inspiration of the character of Liza Doolittle in *Pygmalion*

Stead also was a confidant of world figures such as Cecil Rhodes, and campaigned against British involvement in the Boer War. Whether with the Tsar of Russia or the President of the United States, Stead was a tireless worker for peace and was twice nominated for the Nobel Peace Prize.

Other well known passengers included Colonel John Jacob Astor IV returning to New York after his honeymoon with his young wife Madeleine. The *Titanic* would carry 22 honeymoon couples on this first voyage. Isa and Isidor Straus who had founded Macy's department store in New York, were returning after a holiday. Many of these passengers were accompanied by their servants and their pets. John Jacob Astor brought his Airedale terrier, *Kitty*.

Representing the White Star Line was the chairman, J. Bruce Ismay who would occupy the suite which had been allocated to the ship's American owner J. Pierpoint Morgan. Morgan's company, International Mercantile Marine (I.M.M.), owned White Star, but he withdrew from the voyage at the last moment claiming he was unwell.

First Class passengers went aboard by the main entrance on 'B' deck where they were welcomed by Chief Steward Andrew Latimer and shown to their cabins. Many of these passengers would be met by stewards who had served them on previous trips and who they had requested as their steward to serve them on the *Titanic*. The accommodation on 'A', 'B' and 'C' decks was for the exclusive use of First Class passengers. The most expensive suites on the *Titanic* cost £870, but this price included a free inside cabin for the occupant's servants.

Up on the Bridge Captain E. J. Smith was joined by the harbour pilot George Bowyer who would guide the *Titanic* out into Southampton Water. They talked amongst other things about 'the suction effect' that these huge new liners the *Olympic* and the *Titanic* could cause when they came close to another vessel. At the age of 62, Captain Smith would retire after commanding the *Titanic* on her maiden voyage.

Just before noon the *Titanic* gave three loud blasts on her horn. The tugs took up the slack on the hawsers, the lines were released from the quayside. Slowly the great liner was moved into River Test turning circle where the tugs turned her through 90° to face the sea. As it was low tide this was a difficult manoeuvre with little room for error.

The *Titanic* moved forward under her own power, her great engines and propellers caused a great deal of turbulence in the water. As she passed the moored *Oceanic* and the *New York* the great displacement of water caused the mooring ropes on the *New York* to snap with a loud crack which some said 'sounded like gunshots'. As the *Titanic* gathered speed she pulled the *New York* towards her until the two vessels were only a few feet apart and a collision seemed inevitable. Fortunately the tug *Vulcan* was able to get a line onto the *New York* and pull her clear at the last moment. By the time the *New York* had been made secure, more than an hour had passed during which the *Titanic* was stopped with her starboard anchor made ready to be lowered should this be necessary. It is said that some passengers remarked that this start to their journey was not a good omen for the days that lay ahead.

When able to move forward once again the *Titanic* did so with great care, particularly when negotiating the section of Southampton Water where the *Olympic* had collided with HMS *Hawke*, some seven months earlier.

While the ship travelled along Southampton Water, the ship's bugler P. W. Fletcher, went from deck to deck playing *The Roast Beef of Old England*, the traditional meal call on White Star liners to inform passengers that their first meal aboard the new ship was about to be served. Meals were served for all classes at the same time. Breakfast was served from 8.30am to 10.30am, lunch from 1pm. to 2.30pm and dinner from 6pm to 7.30pm. The First Class restaurant stayed open much longer.

Alexander was on duty during all meal hours, and for about an hour before and after every breakfast, lunch and dinner.

The First Class Dining Room, situated on 'D' deck, was the largest room on the *Titanic*. It occupied the entire width of the ship (92 feet) and was 114 feet in length. It could seat over 550 people at one time, its oak furniture giving the appearance of a Jacobean stately home. Towards the forward end and in the middle was the Captain's table, where the Captain would entertain his guests. One feature that distinguished the Dining Saloon on the *Titanic* from that on the *Olympic* was the carpet that covered the floor. "You sank in it up to your knees", was how Baker Reginald Burgess described it.

First Class passengers would meet in the 54 feet long Reception Room before going in to dine. This room also covered the full width of the ship. First Class passengers could also choose to eat in the restaurant on 'B' deck where an extensive a` la carte menu was available. It employed staff from London restaurants, managed by Luigi Gatti, and was open from 8am to 11pm daily. Meals taken here had to paid for separately although any passenger who used this restaurant throughout the voyage was entitled to a rebate of up to £5 from the White Star Line.

The First Class Dining Room on the Olympic.

The menu in the First Class Dining Room was contained in a folder which featured Europa & Columbia *on either side of a radiant white star.*

R.M.S. *TITANIC*
April 10 1912

LUNCHEON

CONSOMMÉ JARDINIERE - HODGE PODGE
FILLETS OF PLAICE
BEEF STEAK & KIDNEY PIE
ROAST SURREY CAPON

FROM THE GRILL

GRILLED MUTTON CHOPS
MASHED, FRIED & BAKED JACKET POTATOES
RICE PUDDING
APPLES MANHATTAN - PASTRY

BUFFET

FRESH LOBSTERS - POTTED SHRIMPS
SOUSED HERRINGS - SARDINES
ROAST BEEF
ROUND OF SPICED BEEF
VIRGINIA & CUMBERLAND HAM
BOLOGNA SAUSAGE - BRAWN
GALANTINE OF CHICKEN
CORNED OX TONGUE
LETTUCE - TOMATOES

CHEESE

CHESHIRE, STILTON, GORGONZOLA, EDAM
CAMEMBERT, ROQUEFORT, ST. IVEL

Iced draught Munich Lager Beer 3d & 6d a Tankard.

The pilot was put off and the *Titanic* headed for Cherbourg with the French tricolour at her foremast. Due to the delay in Southampton it was 6.30pm before the *Titanic* dropped anchor off Cherbourg. The tenders the *Nomadic* and the *Traffic* brought out a further 274 First, Second and Third Class passengers to join the ship. First and Second

Class passengers travelled on the *Nomadic* while the *Traffic* carried Third Class passengers and the baggage. Among the notable passengers joining the ship were Mrs J. J. Brown (known as Molly to her friends), Benjamin Guggenheim, also Sir Cosmo and Lady Duff Gordon (travelling under the names of Mr. and Mrs. Morgan). Fifteen First Class and seven Second Class passengers disembarked having paid £1-10s and £1 respectively for their cross-Channel tickets. Just after 8pm, the *Titanic* raised anchor and set sail through the night headed for Queenstown (now Cobh) in Ireland.

On the morning of the 11th April, Alexander would have been up early to serve breakfast at 8am in the First Class Saloon.

R.M.S. *TITANIC*

April 11 1912

BAKED APPLES - FRESH FRUIT - STEWED PRUNES
QUAKER OATS - BOILED HOMINY - PUFFED RICE

FRESH HERRINGS
FINDON HADDOCK - SMOKED SALMON
GRILLED MUTTON KIDNEYS & BACON
GRILLED HAM - GRILLED SAUSAGE
LAMB COLLOPS - VEGETABLE STEW
FRIED, SHIRRED, POACHED & BOILED EGGS
PLAIN AND TOMATO OMELETTES TO ORDER
SIRLOIN STEAK & MUTTON CHOPS TO ORDER
MASHED, SAUTÉ & JACKET POTATOES
COLD MEAT

VIENNA & GRAHAM ROLLS
SODA & SULTANA SCONES - CORN BREAD
BUCKWHEAT CAKES
BLACK CURRANT CONSERVE - NARBONNE HONEY
OXFORD MARMALADE
WATERCRESS

At 11.30am on the morning of 11th April the *Titanic* arrived two miles offshore from Queenstown, where she was met by the tenders, the *America*, and the *Ireland*, which brought 113 Third Class and seven Second Class passengers out to the ship. Many of these passengers were emigrating to America to start a new life.

Seven passengers disembarked, having paid £4 for their ticket to Ireland. Also on the tenders when they left, hiding under mailbags, was 24-year-old stoker John Coffey. Never intending to make the journey to New York he had signed on to get a free passage home to Ireland. At 1.30pm, the *Titanic* was again ready to set sail, now with the American flag flying from her foremast. The next landfall for her passengers and crew was to be New York on the morning of the 17th April. Before the *Titanic* left Chief Officer Wilde posted a letter to his sister saying, "I still don't like this ship ....I have a queer feeling about it".

As *Titanic* sailed from Queenstown, Third Class passenger Eugene Patrick Daly played "Erin's Lament" on his uileann, (traditional Irish pipes).

Each morning would start for First Class passengers at 7am with tea, coffee and fruit brought to their cabins together with a copy of the *Atlantic Daily Bulletin*, the *Titanic's* own newspaper. They would then dress in time for the 8am bugle summoning them to breakfast. Meals for both the First and Second Class dining rooms were prepared in the same galleys.

When breakfast over there was time to enjoy the many facilities the *Titanic* had to offer. The choice included a gymnasium, with many different types of exercise machines, a swimming pool (a new feature on liners), a squash court with resident professional and an extensive library for those who were looking for a quieter activity. All these activities were extras, which had to be paid for, the swimming pool costing one shilling each time it was used.

There were no organised activities for passengers in any of the classes; no parties, balls or dances. Passengers were expected to pass the day organising themselves with only mealtimes adhering to a set routine. Many passengers would pass the day reading, writing or playing cards. For the more active a stroll on deck to take the sea air was popular. Another favourite pastime for the First Class passengers was using the Marconi wireless system to send messages to their friends and relations. Passengers paid for their hand-written messages at the rate of 12s 6d for the first 10 words and 9d a word for each additional word (postage of letters in the UK cost 1d in 1912). The messages were sent from the enquiry office to the wireless cabin by pneumatic tube. Incoming messages were dealt with in the same way, being taken by cabin boy to the addressee's cabin or one of the public rooms. Messages regarding the ship were taken directly to the bridge. The Marconi operators Jack Phillips (senior operator) and Harold Bride (junior operator) received a commission depending on the number of passenger messages they transmitted. Passengers wanting to buy souvenirs of their journey could do so from the ship's barber shop which contained a full range of the *Titanic* and White Star Line mementoes. Clear skies and a calm sea made the voyage even more enjoyable for those on board.

Every day, except Sunday, Captain Smith wearing his full dress uniform carried out a thorough inspection of his ship, together with his officers, as he was required to do in White Star Line rules.

The only complaint that passengers in Third Class had was the shortage of baths in their accommodation. There were only two to be shared among more than 700 passengers.

From noon on the 11th April to noon on the 12th April, the *Titanic* travelled 484 miles, and from noon on the 12th April to noon on the 13th April, a further 519 miles. This was less than the *Olympic* had covered during the same period on her maiden voyage, but there were still over three days to go before reaching New York. Bruce Ismay was reported to be determined that the *Titanic* would beat the time that the *Olympic* had set.

On the morning of Sunday 14th April W. T. Stead awoke, having been troubled during the night by a strange dream. That night at dinner he told his companions how he had dreamed about "someone throwing cats out of a top storey window".

Mr Stead, as editor of the *Pall Mall Gazette,* had written an article on the 22nd March 1886, entitled *How the Mail Steamer went down in Mid Atlantic, by a Survivor.* This described how an unnamed steamer sank after colliding with another ship and many lives were lost due to a shortage of lifeboats.

In the 1892 Christmas edition of *The Review of Reviews,* Stead wrote a short story called, *From the Old World to the New.* The story told how the White Star liner, the *Majestic,* under the command of Captain E. J. Smith, sails through an Atlantic ice field, coming upon a survivor on the iceberg that sank his liner; the castaway makes his presence known to those on the *Majestic* by telepathy. (The *Majestic* was the ship that the *Titanic* replaced on the Atlantic crossing and which would again be the ship that passengers would use after the loss of the *Titanic*).

Five years later, in 1898, a story called *Futility* (or *The Wreck of the Titan*) was written by a retired merchant navy officer called Morgan Robertson. The *Titan* is described as a huge liner, which on its maiden voyage from Southampton to New York, with 2,000 people on board, hits an iceberg on its starboard side and sinks leaving only 13 survivors. The great loss of life is due to a lack of lifeboats. Both the *Titan* and the *Titanic* sailed in April, had triple screw propellers and a top speed of 24-25 knots. These stories were written many years before the maiden voyage of the *Titanic,* yet uncannily seemed to foretell the disaster.

Sunday morning on White Star liners was normally the time when all passengers and crew would assemble in life jackets at their boat stations, although no drill was called for

The ship's bugler,
P. W. Fletcher, who played
The Roast Beef of Old
England, to summon
passengers to dinner.

that morning of the 14th April. Perhaps it was thought unnecessary on this "practically unsinkable ship" When Mrs. Albert Caldwell asked a deck hand, "Is this ship really unsinkable?", she received the answer, "Even God Himself could not sink this ship."

Or was it because Captain Smith and the owners of the White Star line knew the number of lifeboats was totally inadequate for the number of passengers and crew aboard the liner? The original design for the Olympic class of ship drawn up by the then general manager of Harland and Wolff, Alexander Carlisle, showed provision of 64 lifeboats, this number was first reduced first to 32 and then to 16 lifeboats. By January 1912 when the boats were installed Carlisle no longer worked for Harland and Wolff. The Welin Davits fitted to the *Titanic* could each have lowered three boats in succession but only one boat was fitted. Would the second and third boat have spoiled the ship's appearance or would it have alarmed passengers to think so many boats were necessary? The Board of Trade regulations for lifeboats had remained unchanged since 1894 when ships over 10,000 tons were required to carry life boats and rafts for a total of 962 people. The *Titanic* had in addition to the 16 lifeboats, (capacity 980 people), a further four Englehardt collapsible boats (seating 196 people) giving a total of 1,176 places, well above the required official number but approximately half that of the number on board (2,207) and a third of the ships capacity of 3,547. (It was later calculated that 63 lifeboats would have been necessary to accommodate the *Titanic's* full complement of passengers and crew - Alexander Carlisle's original plan. Whether it would have been possible to launch that number of boats in the time the *Titanic* had available is a matter for conjecture.) Whatever the reason, boat drill did not take place that Sunday morning.

At 9am a message had been received from the Cunard liner, the *Caronia.... Westbound steamers report bergs, growlers and field ice 42° North from 49 to 51° West.* (Growlers are small icebergs hardly visible above the water). The message was taken to the Bridge where Captain Smith posted it on the notice board for his officers.

At 10.30am, Captain Smith led the morning service in the First Class Dining Saloon. Passengers from all classes on the ship could attend and music was provided by the ships orchestra, under the direction of their leader Wallace Hartley. The service finished at 11.30am with everyone singing *Oh God, our Help in Ages Past.* 10 minutes later, The Dutch liner the *Noordam* reported ice in the same position as that reported by the *Caronia*.

On the Saturday evening a fault had developed in the Marconi wireless system and it was not fixed until 5.00am on Sunday morning. In the meantime a large backlog of passengers messages had built up for the two operators Jack Phillips and Harold Bride. At 1.40pm they received an incoming message from the White Star liner the *Baltic*. The message read -"Captain Smith, *Titanic* - Greek steamer *Athinai* reports passing icebergs and large quantities of field ice today in latitude 41.51° North, 49.52° West," very close to the *Titanic's* planned course.

The message was taken to the Bridge were it was handed to Captain Smith. Instead of pinning it on the officers board he took it with him down to lunch where he showed it to Bruce Ismay who put it in his pocket. It was not until 7.15pm when Captain Smith asked for its return that the message was posted on the Bridge.

At 1.45pm Jack Phillip's intercepted a message from the liner the *Amerika* stating that she had "just passed two large icebergs" in a position close to the *Titanics* course. The message was not sent to the Bridge.

During the afternoon of the 14th April there was a marked fall in the air temperature. Most passengers avoided the cold by keeping off the decks; going to read in the ship's library or warming themselves in front of the real coal fires in the First Class cabins.

At 5.00pm the *Titanic* reached what was termed 'the corner', a point 42° North 47° West. From there the ship's course would change from Southwest to almost due west. There was, however, a delay of some 30 minutes before the correction was made. This resulted in the *Titanic* being some ten miles south of the normal shipping lane. Between 5.30pm and 7.30pm the air temperature dropped by a further 10° to a chilly 33° Fahrenheit.

Captain E. J. Smith with Purser Herbert McElroy.

The ship's bugler, P. W. Fletcher, summoned passengers to dinner. Alexander was serving dinner at Purser McIlroys table where W. T. Stead was seated next to Frederick K. Seward, a famous New York lawyer. There were eight men around the table, six of who were English. After telling his dream about cats, Stead loaned Seward a book which he said "would make any reader dream to distraction". He also described to Seward the persecution to which he and Lloyd George were subjected because of their opposition to government policies, such as the war in South Africa.

The meal that Alexander served was as follows:

Mr W. T. Stead,
Alexander last saw him
when he took him a large
cup of coffee in the
Reception Room, just
after dinner

R.M.S. *TITANIC*
April 14 1912

HORS D'OEUVRE VARIES
OYSTERS
CONSOMMÉ OLGA - CREAM OF BARLEY
SALMON, MOUSSELINE SAUCE, CUCUMBER
FILET MIGNONS LILI
SAUTÉ OF CHICKEN, LYONNAISE
VEGETABLE MARROW FARCIE

LAMB, MINT SAUCE
ROAST DUCKLING APPLE SAUCE
SIRLOIN OF BEEF - CHATEAU POTATOES

GARDEN PEAS - CREAMED CARROTS
BOILED RICE
PARMENTIER & BOILED NEW POTATOES
PUNCH ROMAINE
ROAST SQUAB & CRESS
COLD ASPARAGUS VINAIGRETTE
PATE DE FOIE GRAS
CELERY

WALDORF PUDDING
PEACHES IN CHARTREUSE JELLY
CHOCOLATE AND VANILLA ECLAIRS
FRENCH ICE CREAM

The meal comprised of 11 different courses, including dessert. At each course Alexander would have gone to each diner with silver serving platters, always from the left, offering something from each dish. He would also have used his knowledge of the wine trade to suggest appropriate wines to accompany each course. It is likely that the oysters were served raw on the half shell. Oysters must have featured on many First Class menus, as the *Titanic* left Southampton with 1,221 quarts of them! Even though it is not mentioned on the menu, each meal would have ended with baskets of fresh fruit and a selection of cheeses. After the dessert course Alexander would have offered coffee, cigars, port and liqueurs at the table or to those who had returned to the Reception Room. Liqueurs were then referred to as *cordials* and were often poured straight into the coffee. It was for this reason that the cups were served only three quarters-full. Gentlemen would normally retire to the Smoking Room to enjoy their cigars. Before and during the meal, diners would be entertained by a five piece orchestra under the leadership of Wallace Hartley. Diners in the a' la carte restaurant listened to a string trio.

At 7.15pm, First Officer Murdoch ordered Lamp Trimmer Samuel Hemming to make sure the forward hatches were closed, so that no light would interfere with the Lookouts view ahead. The Lookouts had to rely on eyesight alone, as the binoculars, which had been in the crows nest when the ship left Belfast, were now missing. They had not been replaced, even though there were five pairs on the Bridge. Only one ninth of an iceberg is visible above the water and at night they can be can be very difficult to distinguish against a background of sea and sky. This was particularly so in a very calm sea, such as on the night of the 14th April 1912, as there would be no tell tale waves breaking around the base of the berg.

At 7.30pm, Harold Bride overheard an ice warning, sent from the Leyland freighter the *Californian*, reporting "three large bergs five miles south of us." Bride acknowledged the signal and delivered the message to the Bridge.

Captain Smith was a guest that evening at a party, organised by George and Eleanor Widener, in the a` la carte restaurant. Just before 9.00pm he returned to the Bridge. There he spoke to Second Officer Lightoller, who told him that he was concerned that the fresh water tanks might freeze if the temperature dropped much further. There were a great many stars, which Lightoller thought would aid in spotting any ice. At 9.20pm, Captain Smith left the bridge to go to bed, telling Lightoller to inform him if there was any change in the weather conditions. Second Officer Lightoller sent a message to the crow's nest to keep a sharp lookout for ice, particularly small ice and growlers.
The Lookouts, George Symons and Archie Jewell, would be relieved when their watch finished at 10pm.

At 9.40pm, Jack Phillips, alone in the wireless room, received a message from the westbound, SS *Mesaba* -"From *Mesaba* to *Titanic* and all eastbound ships. Ice report

Mr & Mrs W. T. Stead.

in latitude 42° North to 41.25° North, longitude 49° West to 50.30° West. Saw much heavy pack ice and a great number large ice bergs. Also field ice. Weather good, clear." As the *Titanic* was now within range of the Marconi land station at Cape Race in Newfoundland, Phillips continued to give priority to passengers messages, putting the message from the *Mesaba* to one side. It was never delivered to the Bridge, even though the reported ice lay directly in the *Titanic's* path.

At 10.00pm, First Officer Murdoch took command of the Bridge in place of Second Officer Lightoller. Lookouts Frederick Fleet and Reginald Lee, climbed the 50 foot ladder inside the forward mast to reach the crow's nest and were given the message to watch out for ice by Symons and Jewell as they went off duty. The *Titanic* had six Lookouts, who worked in pairs, with two hours on duty and then four hours off. Fleet and Lee would be glad when midnight came, and they could return to the warmth of their cabin.

By now, most of the passengers were in bed but a few, including W. T. Stead, had remained in the reception room after dinner. It was here that Alexander brought him a large cup of coffee, on what was to be the last occasion he ever saw the great man.

At 10.30pm, the freighter the *Rappahannock* sailing eastwards sent a message to the *Titanic* by Morse signal lamp "Have just passed through heavy field ice and several icebergs". The *Titanic* replied "Message received, Thank you, good night."

In his wireless room at 10.55pm, Jack Phillips was still busy transmitting messages to Cape Race. He was suddenly interrupted by a loud signal coming from the *Californian*. Cyril Evans, wireless operator on the *Californian*, was saying "We are stopped surrounded by ice" when Phillip's cut in saying " Keep out ! Shut up! You're jamming my signal". Evans stopped sending and listened to the messages being sent to Cape Race. At 11.30pm, he switched off his set, and went to bed.

The stewards closed down the First and Second Class lounges and Alexander returned to his room at 11.00pm and sat talking to two or three friends. Among them was probably Steward Brown with whom he was great friends. At 11.30pm, tired from a long days work, Alexander went to bed. The ship was now quiet except for the two smoking rooms where the card players and those enjoying a late cigar or drink still remained.

3. "ICEBERG RIGHT AHEAD"

The sea temperature had dropped to 31° F. Some passengers were finding it hard to sleep, as there was more vibration than usual, due to the ship's increased speed. That morning, two further boilers had been lit, and now the *Titanic* was travelling at 22 1/2 knots. In the crow's nest, Frederick Fleet and Reginald Lee were straining their eyes into the distance. When they had come on duty at 10.00pm, the night sky was cloudless and the air was clear but now a slight mist had appeared, which lay in their path. As he stared into the darkness, Fleet suddenly rang the warning bell three times, the signal for something dead ahead. He then picked up the telephone connecting him to the bridge. Sixth Officer James Moody asked "What do you see?" "Iceberg right ahead" replied Fleet. "Thank you" said Moody. The time was 11.40pm.

The iceberg appeared to Fleet and Lee as a great black mass, difficult to distinguish in the haze. They estimated it to be as high as the ship, but not as high as the crow's nest. On the Bridge, First Officer William Murdoch, gave the order to Quartermaster Robert Hitchens, who was at the wheel, "Hard a' starboard." This order meant that the wheel was turned to the starboard (or right hand side of the ship facing the bow), which had the effect of turning the rudder and the ship's direction to the port, or left. At the same time he telegraphed the engine room 'Stop, Full speed astern'. As he did this he pushed the alarm bell which warned those in the engine room that the watertight doors would close in 10 seconds. Then he activated the switch which would automatically close the doors.

On her trials the *Titanic* had taken 850 yards to stop and that was at a speed of 20 knots. Fleet estimated that he had seen the iceberg for the first time when it was less than 500 yards away with the *Titanic* travelling at 22 1/2 knots. Had the engines not been put into reverse the *Titanic* would have turned more quickly to port, but it was too late. Less than a minute after the berg was sighted the *Titanic*, having turned just two degrees to port, scraped her starboard side along the iceberg. As she did so large pieces of ice broke off the berg and fell on the ship's deck.

As the *Titanic* passed the iceberg, Murdoch gave the order "Hard a' port" to try to bring the ship's stern away from the ice but it was too late the damage was done. As the ship had come into contact with the iceberg, the pressure on the metal plates which made up the hull of the ship became intense. Under this pressure the steel rivets which held the plates together gave way causing gaps to open below the waterline.

(Until recently the damage caused by the iceberg was described as, a 'three hundred feet gash', but now in the opinion of two scientists and an ultra sound scan of the *Titanic* wreck, it is believed that damage was limited to six narrow slits totalling an area of about 13 square feet).

Mr. William H. Garzke Jr., a naval architect has led a team of marine forensic experts investigating the disaster. Working with Mr. Garzke, Dr. Timothy Foecke, a metallurgist discovered that the rivets that held the ship's metal plates together were made from brittle steel which made them more likely to break under pressure. Three million rivets were used in the building of the *Titanic*. One of Mr. Garzke's more fanciful claims is that, had the passengers used clothing, bed sheets and mattresses to plug the gaps, most of which were less than an inch wide, then the sinking could have been delayed until the rescue ships had arrived.

In his cabin, Alexander was woken by what he describes as "a shaking sort of noise. The whole ship seemed to shake." He compared it to the noise he had heard on the *Olympic* when it lost a propeller blade. A few seconds later he heard the cry "Watertight door". He got up and dressed and heard someone say that the ship had hit an iceberg. Alexander's accommodation was on the Upper Deck (Deck 'E') on the port-side, amidships. This was the lowest deck on the ship where it was possible to travel the whole length of the ship at one level. In the bow was crew accommodation for the trimmers and some Third Class accommodation. Starboard amidships was taken up with First Class cabins, port amidships were stewards cabins. The Engineers' Mess was further aft. The wide working passageway which linked the bow to the stern along 'E' deck was known to the crew as *The Scotland Road*.

The cry Alexander heard of "watertight doors" could not possibly have been for the closing of the doors in the boiler rooms, but was the warning that the watertight doors in the passageway were about to close. These doors were not operated electronically from the Bridge, but were closed manually.

On the Bridge, First Officer Murdoch was joined by Captain Smith. "What have we struck?" the Captain asked. "An iceberg, Sir" replied Murdoch. He described to the Captain the measures he had already taken, including closing the watertight doors.

Meanwhile in Boiler Room Number Six, the most forward of the ship's boiler rooms on the starboard side, Leading Stoker Frederick Barrett and Second Engineer James Hesketh were confronted by a rush of water, pouring in through a gap two feet above the floor. Hesketh and Barrett got through the watertight door into Boiler Room Number Five before it closed, but Fireman George Beauchamp, who was working to shut the dampers (cut off the supply of air to the boilers), had to climb the emergency ladder connecting the two rooms. The situation in Boiler Room Number Five was not much better, as there was a gash extending from a point two feet aft of the forward bulkhead into the bunker which had been on fire earlier on the voyage. The lights went out and Frederick Barrett went up an escape ladder to collect lanterns. When he returned the lights had come on again. By now Boiler Room Number Six was under eight feet of water.

For the passengers, most of whom were unaware of what was going on far below, the cause of the shudder was still a matter for conjecture. For those who had stayed up for a final cigar or game of cards in the First Class Smoking Room on 'A' Deck, the cause was all too clear. They watched as the iceberg scraped along the starboard side of the ship. When going out onto the deck they saw the pieces of ice that had fallen onto the deck and the iceberg disappearing astern dark against the starlit sky.

Alexander went to the forward part of the ship and out onto the top deck. There he saw about two feet of ice lying in the scuppers on the starboard side. He noticed the brightness overhead and the tremendous number of stars, as well as a slight mist on the water. He didn't stay on the top deck long because he did not regard the situation as serious. Going one deck down he saw the carpenter sounding the forward well and saw that there was a quantity of water in it as the line was pulled up. Suddenly, Alexander realised that things were more serious than he had at first suspected. He returned to his room where he told his friends that he thought they might soon be required to help the passengers. There was never any thought in his head at this stage that they might have to leave the ship, he and his colleagues still believed the *Titanic* to be unsinkable.

There were already quite a few passengers out on the deck when W. T. Stead decided to go and investigate what had happened. "What do they say is the trouble?' asked Stead. "Icebergs" explained Frank Millet, an American painter. "Well" said Stead, "I guess it's nothing serious; I'm going back to my cabin to read."

In his cabin, Bruce Ismay had also been awaked by the scraping sound. Like Alexander his first thoughts were that the *Titanic* had lost a propeller blade. Putting an overcoat over his pyjamas he headed for the bridge where he asked Captain Smith what had happened. The Captain explained that the ship had struck an iceberg. "Is the ship seriously damaged?" asked Ismay. "I'm afraid she is", replied the Captain. His worst fears were soon to be confirmed. Thomas Andrews was summoned to the bridge and together he and Captain Smith made a 10 minute inspection of the damage. The first five compartments were filling, making the bow sink lower. As the watertight bulkhead between Boiler Rooms Six and Five only extended up as far as 'E' deck, the water would eventually flow over the top and as the bow dropped still further, the water would fill Boiler Room Four, then Three, then Two.

Andrews knew the *Titanic* was doomed. He explained to Captain Smith how the *Titanic* could float with any two of her 16 watertight compartments flooded. She could float with any three of her first five compartments flooded, even with all of her first four compartments full. With her first five compartments full she would sink. "How long have we got ?" asked Captain Smith. " One and a half hours, maybe two", Andrews replied.

Fourth Officer Joseph Boxall, who had gone below on the starboard side to determine the extent of the damage, reported to the Captain that water was coming into the lower

Mail Sorting Room and that bags of mail were being moved to the deck above. Captain Smith asked Boxall to calculate the ship's position.

The time was now five past midnight and the Captain ordered Chief Officer Henry Wilde to organise the uncovering of the lifeboats and Boxall to summon any off-duty officers to the Bridge. Sixth Officer Moody was put in charge of lifeboat assignment (each crew man was assigned a boat and was expected to row passengers to safety, but there had been no lifeboat drill and many were unsure about their duties). First Officer Murdoch was to organise the muster of passengers although it was thought unnecessary to alarm them at this stage.

Alexander and his friends saw Steerage (Third Class) passengers coming from their accommodation at the front part of the ship. They were wearing lifebelts and carrying their luggage with them. "We laughed at these fellows at first (single male passengers in Third Class had accommodation in the bow, while single women in Third Class were accommodated in the stern) and thought they were unnecessarily scared", said Alexander. "But when we saw some of them were wet through we knew there must be a lot of water in their quarters".

Taking the piece of paper on which Fourth Officer Boxall had written the ship's position, 41.46° North, 50.14° West, Captain Smith headed for the Marconi wireless cabin. Inside the cabin the two men seemed unaware of the gravity of the situation. Bride had decided to help Phillips around midnight, even though his shift didn't start until 2.00am, as there was still such a backlog of passengers messages to send. Bride had hardly taken over the headphones when the Captain entered the cabin. "We've struck an iceberg, be ready to call for assistance when I tell you". Minutes later the Captain was back. "Send the call for assistance". Phillips, who had now taken the headphones from Bride, asked if he should use the regulation distress call. "Yes", the Captain replied, "send at once". At 12.15am Phillips started tapping out the letters C Q D (Come Quick Danger) followed by the *Titanic's* call letters *MGY*.

Alexander heard the order that the crew were being mustered from a night watchman. "All hands in the saloon". While he was getting ready the second steward came down and said "Every man get on deck at once; put on warm clothing and lifebelts". He added "Don't leave a man here, or else he may never come out of it perhaps". Alexander and those with him dressed, put there lifebelts on and went up onto the deck. When they reached the deck they were told to get to their boat stations. Alexander had to pass many of the First Class cabins where he saw the bedroom stewards assisting the passengers get their lifebelts on. He did not however see W. T. Stead in cabin C89 being assisted by Bedroom Steward Andrew Cunningham.

At 12.25am Harold Cottam, wireless operator on the Cunard liner the *Carpathia*, bound for the Mediterranean, was coming to the end of his shift. Having received the distress signal from the *Titanic*, Cottam took it straight to Captain Arthur Rostron. The

Carpathia was some 58 miles from the *Titanic* and even at maximum speed would take four hours to reach the stricken liner. The *Carpathia* was the nearest ship to respond to the *Titanic's* distress calls. Others, who included her sister ship the *Olympic,* 500 miles away and travelling westwards, heard the calls but were too far away to be able to assist. First Class passengers had begun to assemble with their lifebelts and were able to listen to Wallace Hartley and his musicians playing rag-time music in an effort to keep everyone cheerful and to ensure that no panic set in.

At 12.45am, the first lifeboat was ready to be launched. The order had gone out from Captain Smith that women and children should be put in the lifeboats. First Officer Murdoch had taken charge of launching the odd numbered lifeboats on the starboard side while Chief Officer Wilde controlled the launching of the even numbered boats on the port side.

The first boat lowered was Boat Seven, with only 28 people, in a boat that could carry 65. At this time the first distress rockets were fired. In all, the *Titanic* fired eight distress rockets which exploded at 800 feet scattering white stars. (It was the practice, despite the invention of wireless communication, for ships to fire 'company signals' when approaching other vessels at night. These would identify the shipping line not the identity of the vessel. This has been suggested as a reason that ships in the vicinity of the *Titanic* did not respond to the distress signals even though no company used only white rockets. The White Star company signal was two green rockets.) Fourth Officer Boxall reported seeing the lights of a vessel approach the *Titanic* to within five or six miles. Despite signalling with a Morse lamp the vessel failed to respond and eventually vanished. Was this the *Californian,* whose wireless operator had gone to bed, and was now stopped waiting for dawn to safely proceed through the ice field, or another vessel-the sailing barque the *Samson* which had been illegally sealing off the Canadian coast? Just before his death in 1962 the Chief Officer of the *Samson* swore under oath that he and his ship were within eyesight of the *Titanic.* When he saw the rockets he thought it was a signal from a fisheries protection vessel to heave to and be searched, so he sailed away in case his illegal cargo was discovered. The *Samson* had no radio. The true story is further complicated by records which have been found placing the *Sansom* in port in Iceland at the time of the sinking. Alexander describes seeing a light which he believed to be a steamer, and rowing towards it, but not getting any closer, and finally the light disappearing.

On the port-side Boat Four was lowered from the Boat Deck to the Promenade Deck where Second Officer Lightoller intended to load passengers through the windows on the deck's forward screen. The windows were closed and had to be cranked open. It took some time to open them and Lightoller went to load other boats leaving several notable First Class passengers waiting.

The first boat launched on the port-side was Boat Six, at 12.55am. This boat, capable of carrying 65, held 28 people.

Under the command of quartermaster Robert Hitchens it contained the Lookout Frederick Fleet, who had first spotted the iceberg, Molly Brown and other ladies. Major Arthur Peuchen, an experienced yachtsman, volunteered to row as there was no other seaman in the boat. He was one of very few male passengers, in the boats lowered under the supervision of Second Officer Lightoller.

At the same time on the starboard side Boat Five was lowered under the command of Third Officer H. J. Pitman. Bruce Ismay not satisfied with the rate at which the boats were being lowered, tried to intervene, but was promptly told by Fifth Officer Lowe not to interfere. Boat Five left with 41 aboard, a mixture of male and female passengers and crew. At 1.00am Boat Three left with 32 aboard including 11 crew.

First Officer Murdoch then decided to launch Emergency Boat One. This boat with a capacity of forty left the *Titanic* with 12 aboard, including seven crew. The other five passengers were Sir Cosmo Duff-Gordon, his wife Lucille, her maid, and two American men. It may well have been in Murdoch's mind that the under-filled boats would be able to pick up survivors from the water after the *Titanic* had gone down and that time was very limited in getting the boats away. There was also a reluctance on the part of some passengers to leave the liner in a small boat on the Atlantic on a freezing cold night.

On the port-side, at the same time, Boat Eight was lowered away. It was in this boat that Mrs Ida Straus turned down a place as it meant leaving her husband Isidor. "We have lived together we will die together" she said.

4. LIFEBOAT 13

At 1.15am, water had reached the name *Titanic* on the ship's bow. Two more boats, Boat Nine and Boat 10, were lowered at 1.20am containing 56 and 55 people respectively.

Alexander was by then on the Boat Deck where he assisted in getting his lifeboat, Boat 11, swung out over the ship's side. He then went down to 'A' deck where he helped to load the boat with women and children. This boat was loaded with 70 people, 10 more than its capacity. Of these, three were First Class female passengers, three were male passengers, nine were crew (including five stewards and one stewardess) together with 55 Second and Third Class women and children. Due to the flat calm sea it was difficult to unhook the boats from the falls (lowering ropes). According to Alexander, First Officer Murdoch had ordered the boat to be in the charge of Steward C. D. MacKay, but according to other witnesses, Quartermaster Humphries was in charge.

Following this Alexander then went to assist in the loading of Boat 13 with what he estimated to be about 35 women and children. He said, "We shouted for more women but there were none forthcoming". This was not entirely surprising as knowledge of what was going on was limited to a small area around each boat. Alexander then went on to say, "We had a few First Class male passengers in".

In fact Boat 13 had only one First Class male passenger, Dr. Washington Dodge, who had earlier seen his wife and son off in Boat Five, choosing to stay rather than take his place with other First Class wives and their husbands in that boat. Dining Room Steward Frederick Dent Ray noticed him standing him by the lifeboat and after discovering that his wife and child were already off called out "You had better get in here". Ray had served at the doctor's table on both the *Olympic* and the *Titanic* and was one of the reasons that the Dodge family were making this trip. Mr. Lawrence Beesley, a science teacher from Dulwich College travelling Second Class, jumped into the boat when it was level with the Promenade Deck from the Boat Deck.

Most of the other male passengers in the boat, were from the Third Class including several Swedes and one Chinese, Mr Choong Foo. Whether he was allowed in or whether he hid in the boat is unclear, but his discovery caused great anger amongst those women who had left husbands on the ship. Miss Millvina Dean, was later told by her mother that the other women were so annoyed that a Chinese man was in the boat, when their own men couldn't get in, that they wanted to throw him overboard. Thankfully they thought better of it. Millvina, at nine weeks old, was the youngest

*Lawrence Beesley,
occupant of Boat 13*

*Estimates of how many people were in each lifeboat and which boat they were in, change with each piece of new evidence. If there is proof that any person or persons mentioned in Lifeboat 13, were actually in another boat, then this will be acknowledged in later editions.

Georgetta Dean, with
Millvina (baby) & Bertram.
Occupants of Boat 13.

passenger on the *Titanic*. She was travelling with her father and mother Bertram and Georgetta Dean and her 18 month old brother, also called Bertram. The Dean family were emigrating to America where Bertram Dean was to open a tobacconist's shop in Kansas City. He had sold his London pub to help pay for the family's Third Class tickets on the *Titanic*. It was Bertram Dean's quick thinking that got his family from the depths of the ship, through the crowds of terrified passengers to where Boat 13 was being loaded. Georgetta was found a place in the boat and little Bertram. The baby, Millvina, was placed in a mail sack and passed down by members of the crew until she was safely in the boat. Georgetta's last words to her husband were "Hope to see you later". She never did.

Miss Ruth Elizabeth Becker was travelling with her mother and her younger brother and sister, her father having stayed to work as a missionary in India. They were returning to America as her brother Richard had been unwell. Ruth had seen the others leave in Boat 11. As her mother realised that Ruth was not in the boat she cried, "Ruth, get in another boat". Ruth approached Boat 13 and asked Sixth Officer James Moody if she could get in. Moody picked up 12 year old Ruth and put her in the boat. Miss Elizabeth Dowdell was nurse to 5 year old Virginia Emmanuel, and was escorting her to her grandparent's home in New York.

Mary Davis and Lucy Ridsdale shared a Second Class cabin. Mary had first been told there was no danger after the collision, and had gone back to bed. A few minutes later she was told that the ship was sinking and she quickly got dressed. Lucy Ridsdale had a club foot and Mary had to help her make her way to the Boat Deck. Crewmen helped them into Boat 13.

Daniel Buckley had joined the *Titanic* at Queenstown. He was asleep in a communal Third Class cabin near the bow when the collision took place and awoke to find the cabin ankle deep in water. Buckley later described how he and other male passengers climbed into Boat 13. Many of the other men were dragged out but Buckley remembered a woman covering him in a ladies shawl and so he remained in the boat when it was lowered.

Johan Svensson was just 14 years old, when he boarded *Titanic* in Southampton as a Third Class passenger. His father and one of his sisters were already in America and the rest of his family in Sweden intended to follow. As *Titanic* was sinking he made his way to the Boat Deck. The first two lifeboats he went to refused to let him in, before finally, on his third attempt, he was allowed into Boat 13.

Lowering was about to start when Albert and Sylvia Caldwell, teachers from a Christian college in Siam, reached the boat. When Mrs. Caldwell had boarded Mr. Caldwell then passed a bundle to Steward Ray sitting in the stern. It contained the Caldwell's ten month old son, Alden. Albert Caldwell then climbed in near the bow. (In November 1998, Christie's of London auctioned a gold half hunter watch which

Mr. Caldwell gave to a coxswain just before he and his family boarded the lifeboat. Both the watch and the coxswain survived the sinking.)

The crew in Boat 13 included Leading Fireman Frederick Barrett and Fireman Beauchamp, who in Boiler Room Number Six, had been among the first to experience the damage caused by the iceberg. Frederick Barrett had stayed in Boiler Room Five together with Engineers Harvey and Shepard. Shepard broke his leg falling into an open man-hole. Suddenly there was a rush of water as the forward bulkhead gave way. As Frederick Barrett climbed the escape ladder he saw Engineer Harvey swept away as he tried to save his colleague. Boat 13 also contained Lookout Reginald Lee who had been in the crow's nest when the iceberg was first spotted.

When the boat was filled, Alexander describes how he and another man(probably Saloon Steward George Knight) were ordered by an officer (Sixth Officer James Moody) to get in and help row the boat. As Alexander said, "I happened to be one of the fortunate ones to be ordered in". In all there were seven stewards in Boat 13, including Assistant Steward Walter Williams who jumped from the deck and Glory Hole Steward William Wright.

Paul Maugé, from the ship's a` la carte restaurant, jumped 10 feet into the boat as it was being lowered. Working for Luigi Gatti, Maugé, and Chef Rousseau who was with him, were neither crew nor passengers. They were not wearing their uniforms so were allowed onto the boat deck. Maugé told Rousseau to jump, but the chef was too fat and the leap too far and so Maugé jumped without him Someone on a lower deck tried to drag him out but he managed to stay in the boat. It was the last time he ever saw Rousseau.

Boat 13 (capacity 65 persons), was lowered at 1.40am and was the 13th boat to leave the *Titanic*. There were only 27 women and children among the estimated 62 people* it contained. More than half of the men in the boat were members of the crew.

The filling of Boat 13 appears to have been conducted in an organised and orderly manner with very little panic, considering how low the *Titanic* was in the water, with her bow submerged and a pronounced list to starboard.

The only account to differ on the filling of this boat was this rather sensational one given by Dr. Washington Dodge in *The Bulletin* San Francisco April 19th 1912.

"As the excitement began I saw an officer of the *Titanic* shoot down two steerage passengers who were endeavouring to reach the lifeboats. I have learned since that twelve of the steerage passengers were shot altogether, one officer shooting down six. The first-cabin men and women behaved with great heroism."

Dr. Dodge went on to describe how he was recognised by Steward Ray, with whom he had crossed the Atlantic on the *Olympic*. The article went on to describe how the steerage passengers were being shot down and some of the steerage passengers were stabbing right and left in an endeavour to reach the boat.

George W. Beauchamp, fireman occupant of Boat 13.

Reginald R. Lee, lookout occupant of Boat 13.

The boat was filled on one side with 20 to 30 children and a few women. All in the boat were panic stricken and screaming. The steward (Ray) had been ordered to take charge of the thirteenth, and, seizing Dodge, pushed him into the boat, exclaiming that he needed his help in caring for his helpless charges.

Dr Dodge said that when the boats were drawing away from the ship they could hear the orchestra playing *Lead Kindly Light*, and rockets going up from the *Titanic* in the wonderfully clear night. "We could see from the distance that two boats were being made ready to be lowered. The panic was in the steerage, and it was in that part of the ship that shooting was made necessary."

It is difficult to understand how this account could be so different from the others. Perhaps it was just sensationalist journalism?

Alexander when asked about whether there was any actual shooting replied, "The chief officer I think it was, shot one of the Italian waiters belonging to the restaurant because he got into a boat and would not come out of it when told to do so. I think another officer fired his revolver to frighten some foreigners who were looking over the side and intended to jump into a boat as it was being lowered."

Boat 13, made unsteady progress towards the sea tilting sometimes towards the bow and sometimes towards the stern. As the boat was lowered it was in danger of being swamped by water coming from the condenser exhaust and people had to be moved to get at the oars which were still lashed to the seats. Once the oars were freed they could be used to push the boat away from the gush of water. When they reached the water, their problems were not yet over. The flow of water from the condenser had taken them towards the stern of the *Titanic* directly under where Boat 15 was now being lowered. Yelling at the men still on board to stop lowering, their cry was taken up by those on Boat 15. There was still no rise and fall in the sea which would enable those in Boat 13 to release the lowering tackle, so deciding desperate measures were needed, Leading Fireman Fred Barrett cut the stern falls (lowering ropes) while Seaman Robert Hopkins did the same in the bow. Alexander said, "The men who did the lowering of the boats are worthy of the greatest praise for the admirable manner in which they worked."

Boat 13 then pulled away from the *Titanic* into safety. The performance of stewards as oarsmen, a job for which they had never been trained, was often far from perfect. Dr. Washington Dodge remarked "They could no more row than I could serve dinner". Most boats had four at the oars but the shortage of trained seamen and the absence of any lifeboat drill did not help the situation.

Boat 13 in the water,
with Boat 15 directly above.

Leading Fireman Fred Barrett who had taken charge in Boat 13 described the *Titanic* as looking like "a great lighted theatre". He wished he still had the soup he had been warming when the collision had occurred, as he sat shivering in the freezing air. He turned down the offer of a wrap as he felt there were women in the boat with a greater need. The woman next to Lawrence Beesley who held a crying baby asked him to feel if the baby's feet were outside its blanket. He recognised her voice as Miss Hilda Slayter with whom he had sat at the Assistant Purser's table in the Second Class Dining Room. They discovered in talking that they had a mutual friend living in Ireland.

On the port-side Second Officer Charles Lightoller continued to supervise the loading of boats not allowing any male passengers to board. He was joined by Fifth Officer Lowe and Sixth Officer Moody for the launching of Boats 14 and 16. Lowe remarked to Moody that none of the recently launched boats had contained a officer. "You go" said Moody. Lowe filled and then boarded Boat 14 while Moody went to fill Boat 16. In neither boat was there a male passenger. As Boat 14 was being lowered Lowe noticed some men who looked as if they were going to jump into the boat. He fired his revolver along the side of the ship and the men did not jump.

The last boat on the starboard side, the Collapsible Englehardt Boat 'C', had been attached to the davits used by Boat One. Lowered at 1.40am under the direction of Chief Officer Wilde the boat contained women and children. Some reports say that Purser McElroy had to fire his pistol, after some men climbed aboard and had to be hauled out, by other male passengers. Just before the boat was lowered Bruce Ismay and William Carter stepped into it.

Crowds of people were now moving towards the stern away from the ever rising water, Boat Two was lowered at 1.45am with only 25 people on board under the command of Fourth Officer Boxall.

Soon afterwards Boat Four, its wealthy passengers having waited over an hour while the problem with the windows was being sorted out, was ready for lowering. Second Officer Lightoller stood, one foot in Boat Four, with the other on the window sill, while John Joseph Astor helped his pregnant wife into the boat and asked if he could join her. When told he could not he asked for the number of the boat and then gave his wife his gloves. Lightoller also tried to stop 13 year old Jack Ryerson, but when his father intervened, the boy was allowed in the boat with his mother. No other male passenger was allowed in this boat. The 40 occupants of Boat Four were now just 15 feet from the water as the *Titanic* had sunk so low.

There was just one usable boat left on the *Titanic*, the Collapsible 'D'. It was fitted into the empty davits of Boat Two. Just 47 places remained for over 1,500 people still on board. The crew locked arms around the boat only allowing women and children through.

Dr Washington Dodge,
First Class passenger
occupant of Boat 13.

Fireman William Major (standing)
occupant of Boat 13.

Two small boys were handed through by their father and placed in the boat. He said his name was Hoffman, but he was in fact Michel Navratil and the boys were his sons Edmund and Michel Navratil who he had kidnapped from his estranged wife. When Boat 'D' left at 2.05am with 44 people on board, water was already pouring onto the forward end of 'A' deck as the *Titanic* tilted further forward.

A steward saw Thomas Andrews in the First Class Smoking Room at 2.00am. He was standing looking at the painting above the fireplace entitled *Plymouth Harbour*, his lifebelt lay on a table.

Captain Smith made his way to the wireless cabin at 2.10am to release Phillips and Bride from their duties. Since 12.15am when the first distress message was sent out, contact had been made with a number of ships including the *Mount Temple* (49 miles away), *Frankfort* (153 miles) *Birma* (70 miles), *Baltic* (243 miles), *Virginian* (170 miles), *Carpathia* (58 miles) and the land station at Cape Race.

At 12.45am Captain Smith had come to the wireless room and asked what message they were sending. *CQD*, Phillips had replied. "Send *SOS*", suggested Bride. "It's the new call and it may be your last chance to send it". This made both operators laugh for at this stage they could not fully understand the desperate situation the ship was in. Phillips sent *SOS* which was received by her sister ship the *Olympic*. By 1.45am when the *Carpathia* received the message 'Engine room full up to the boilers' it was realised that none of the ships coming to their aid would reach them before the *Titanic* had gone down. At 2.10am Captain Smith said "Men you have done your full duty. You can do no more, abandon your cabin. It's every man for himself".

When the Captain left, Phillips continued to send. Bride went into his sleeping quarters to collect some personal belongings only to return and find a stoker trying to take Phillips lifebelt. Bride grabbed the man and knocked him to the floor. They ran from the cabin to the roof of the officers quarters where Bride helped those trying to free Collapsible Boat 'B'.

Plan of the Titanic's *Boat Deck*
showing position of Boat 13.

5. "A BLAZE OF LIGHT FROM STEM TO STERN"

The musicians, playing under the leadership of Wallace Hartley, had played cheerful ragtime tunes in the First Class lounge soon after the collision. They then moved first to the Boat Deck foyer, and finally to the deck itself as the situation worsened. Towards the end the mood changed and they played more sombre music. Whether the last tune they played was the hymn *Nearer my God to Thee* or the waltz *Songe d' Automne* which was very popular in 1912, is uncertain. Not one member of the band survived the sinking. When asked if he heard the band playing *Nearer my God to Thee*, Alexander replied that the band had been playing when he left the ship but at the time the *Titanic* sank he was nearly half a mile off and could not tell for certain what was being played due to the awful cries of the people.

This is how Alexander described the final moments of the *Titanic*.
"We then lay on our oars and watched. We could see the *Titanic* gradually sinking by the head. Her forward 'E' deck ports were under water, and we could see the lights gradually go out on the 'E' deck as she settled down. All her other lights were burning brilliantly and she looked a blaze of light from stem to stern. We watched her like this for some time, and then suddenly she gave a plunge forward and all the lights went out. Her stern went right up in the air; there were two or three explosions and it appeared to me the stern part came down again and righted itself. Immediately after there were terrible cries for help. They were awful and heartrending.
Soon after this we sighted a light which we thought was a steamer and which I still believe was one. We pulled towards it but we did not appear to get any nearer to it, and after a time the light disappeared."

Alexander's description of *Titanic* being "a blaze of light from stem to stern" was due to the bravery of the 36 Engineers who kept the ship's lighting system working until two minutes before she sank. They did this by switching over from the main to the emergency dynamos which were housed in the fourth (dummy) funnel. Not one Engineer was saved and the same fate befell the five postal clerks who were in one of the first areas to be flooded in the bow of the ship. They stayed guarding their sacks of mail until it was too late for them to escape.

His description of the stern of the ship coming down and righting itself is consistent with *Titanic* breaking into two parts before its descent to the sea bed. The bow section, filled with water, broke away and sank first, followed by the stern section, righting itself, and then as it too filled quickly with water, rose to a vertical position before it slid beneath the surface.

Wallace Hartley,
Titanic *Bandmaster*

James P. Moody,

sixth officer

Lawrence Beesley described what he observed from Boat 13 in the following way:

"The starlight night was beautiful, but as there was no moon it was not very light. The sea was as calm as a pond. There was just a gentle heave as the boat dipped up and down in the swell. It was an ideal night apart from the bitter cold.

In the distance the *Titanic* looked enormous. Her length and her great bulk were outlined in black against the starry sky. Every porthole was blazing with light. It was impossible to think that anything could be wrong with such a leviathan were it not for that ominous tilt downward in the bows, where the water was up to the lowest row of portholes.

At about two o'clock we observed her settling very rapidly with the bows and bridge completely under water. She slowly tilted straight on end with the stern vertically upwards. As she did so the lights in the cabins and the saloons, which had not flickered for one moment since we left, died out, flashed once more, and then went out altogether.

At the same time the machinery broke loose and roared down through the vessel with a groaning rattle that could be heard for miles. It was the weirdest sound, surely, that could be heard in the middle of the ocean. It was not quite the end. To our amazement she remained in that upright position for a time, which I estimate as five minutes.

It was certainly for some minutes that we watched 150 feet of the *Titanic* towering up above the level of the sea, looming black against the sky. Then with a quite slanting dive she disappeared below the water. Our eyes had looked for the last time on the gigantic vessel in which we had set sail from Southampton.

There then fell on our ears that a human being ever heard - the cries of hundreds of our fellow human beings, struggling in the icy waters, crying for help with a cry that we knew could not be answered. We longed to return to pick up some of those who were swimming, but this would have meant the swamping of our boat and the loss of us all."

No one is sure of what fate befell W. T. Stead. After leaving the First Class Smoking Room, Stead and Major Archibald Butt, President Taft's military aide, who was returning after delivering a personal message from President Taft to the Pope, were seen working together putting women and children in the last of the lifeboats. According to Victor Pierce Jones (W. T. Stead's biographer), when the last lifeboat left, Butt's nerve snapped and he shot himself. The last sighting of Stead was claimed by Miss Hilda Slater who said she saw Stead and Colonel Astor, clinging to a raft trying to help others, until they released their hold and sank. (Stead's body was never recovered but that of John Joseph Astor was found, crushed by the falling of the forward funnel). Stead was a strong swimmer and could have reached a lifeboat. He had already given away his lifebelt according to those last to see him.

Others prepared to meet their fate in other ways. Benjamin Guggenheim and his secretary had put on their best evening clothes. "We are dressed in our best and are prepared to go down like gentlemen". Steward Henry Etches recalled him being offered a place in a lifeboat but refusing saying. "I will not go. No woman shall remain unsaved because I was a coward. If I don't turn up, tell my wife I have done my best in doing my duty".

After saying farewell to his wife Madeleine, John Joseph Astor went to the kennels on 'F' deck to release his Airedale, *Kitty*, and the other dogs.

Chief Baker Charles Joughin had been asleep when he heard the collision with the iceberg. He sent each of his staff of 13 bakers with four loaves each to provision the lifeboats. He then returned to his cabin where he had a bottle of whisky. After a drink he went to his boat, Boat 10, at 12.30 am. Joughin found it difficult to persuade women to go into the boat and so in his own words he "threw" them in. He was down to command this boat but as there were plenty of men to handle it already he decided to get out. To go he said "would have set a bad example". Instead he went back to his cabin and had another drink, even though the water was coming through his cabin door and covering his shoes. By the time he got back to the deck all the boats were gone so he began throwing deck chairs through the windows of the promenade deck. After he had thrown about 50 chairs overboard he returned to the pantry this time for water. Suddenly cups and plates crashed off the shelves around him as the *Titanic* gave a sudden lurch. Running out of the pantry he made his way towards the stern of the ship. He climbed over the starboard rail and as the stern rose in the air and the deck listed too steeply to stand on, he walked along the outside of the ship holding onto the rail until he stood on the stern of the ship some 150 feet up in the air. The time was 2.15am when he took his watch off and put it in his pocket. Suddenly the stern section of the *Titanic* started its final dive and as he reached the water Joughin stepped off. Wearing his lifebelt he paddled around in the wreckage for over an hour until in the first light of dawn he paddled over to the upturned Collapsible 'B' which had been washed off the decks when the *Titanic* went down. Although there was no room on the upturned hull an old friend from the kitchen held out a hand and Joughin hung on until the arrival of the Boats 12 and Four, who took him on board. When he was picked up he claimed to have felt colder than when he had been in the freezing water.

Another occupant of the upturned Collapsible Boat 'B' was the Marconi operator Harold Bride. As the boat was washed from the deck of the *Titanic*, Bride was washed off with it only to find himself underneath the upturned boat. As the forward funnel fell the boat was washed some 30 feet away from the sinking ship. After some 45 minutes underneath, breathing in an air pocket Bride succeeded in getting on top of the upturned boat. Once there he was asked by Second Officer Lightoller about which ships he had managed to contact that were coming to their rescue. Bride's colleague Phillip's had also succeeded in reaching the same boat but died of exposure during the night.

Charles Joughin,
chief baker

Harold Sydney Bride,

junior wireless operator

One of Alexander's great friends was the steward Edward Brown. He described to Alexander how he was saved and the last he saw of Captain Smith. When asked about rumours that the Captain had shot himself, Alexander said "there was no truth in that. He was not the sort of man to shoot himself." Edward Brown, said that he was washed off the Bridge as the forward funnel fell, and the Captain was on the Bridge at the time, saying to the other stewards around him, "Do what you can for yourselves boys".

Brown had been assisting in trying to free the other Collapsible Boat 'A' from the roof of the officers quarters. The sides of the boat were never fully raised and as it was washed off the decks of the *Titanic,* it became swamped. Brown managed to get into the boat and stood in over a foot of freezing water until boat 14 under the command of Fifth Officer Lowe picked him up. Also able to get into Boat 'A' after being in the water was a young tennis player Richard Norris Williams. He was wearing a large fur coat which he had put on over his lifejacket. Standing in the freezing water, at least three occupants of this boat died before Boat 14 arrived.

Lowe had first tied five of the boats, Boats Four, 10, 12, 14 and 'D' together, then he transferred 55 from Boat 14 to the other boats. Choosing seamen who could row, he took Boat 14 back to look for survivors. It was after 3am before Lowe recovered Steward John Stewart, passenger William Hoyt (who died within an hour), Bath Attendant Harold Phillimore, and a Japanese passenger roped to a door, who at first Lowe believed to be dead. Once in the boat the man revived and even insisted in helping with the rowing. As day broke Lowe saw the swamped Boat 'A' and picked up those of its occupants that were still alive.

In Boat One, with only 12 occupants, Lady Duff Gordon turned to her secretary after the *Titanic* went down and remarked, "There is your beautiful night-dress gone". "Never mind your night-dress, madam, at least you have got your life" said Fireman Robert Pusey. Then turning to Sir Cosmo he said, "I suppose you have lost everything". "Of course" said Sir Cosmo. "But you can get some more", continued Pusey. "We have lost our kit and the company won't give us any more, also our pay stops from tonight." "Don't worry about that", said Sir Cosmo. "I will give you a fiver each to get a new kit". Some afterwards saw this as an inducement for the crew not to return to pick up survivors.

In Boat 13, Fireman Beauchamp shivered in his thin jumper but refused an extra coat offered by an elderly lady, insisting it went to a young Irish girl instead. When he had left his cabin, Steward Ray had picked up six handkerchiefs. He handed them out giving instructions to tie knots in each corner. He described it as crowning six heads. As the night wore on another crewman remarked "This is no joke we may knock about here days before we are picked up, if at all." A stoker remarked on the sea being as flat as a reservoir and thought of times he had spent on Regents Park Lake. "It reminds me of a blooming picnic" he said.

In Boat Four, Miss Gertrude Hippach watched the shooting stars, and said she had never seen so many. She recalled a legend that every shooting star is someone dying. Many of the women in the boats objected to the men smoking. First Class ladies were not accustomed to seeing men, particularly crew, smoking in their presence.

Alexander describes how they pulled on their oars during the night, keeping in touch with other boats. There was no lantern in Boat 13 and there was the fear that they would drift off and not be found. Stoker Frederick Barrett sat up suddenly in the stern of Boat 13 as he heard the sound of the *Carpathia* firing rockets. "That was a cannon" he exclaimed to the others.

At 3.30am the *Carpathia's* rockets were sighted. Instead of her normal speed of 14 1/2 knots she had raced through the ice to get to the survivors at a speed of 17 1/2 knots. Alexander saw the lights of the *Carpathia* just before dawn. They waited for daylight and began rowing towards their rescue ship. Alexander describes how he found they "were practically surrounded by ice; one iceberg as large as the Isle of Wight lay close by us."

In Boat Three, young Douglas Spedden lay clutching his white toy bear called "Polar". He was asleep on the lap of his nanny, Elizabeth Burns, who he called "Muddie Boons". Suddenly at daybreak he opened his eyes and seeing the ice field all around their boat, he exclaimed, "Oh Muddie, look at the beautiful North Pole with no Santa Claus on it."

As dawn broke, a thin, pale, crescent moon appeared near the horizon. Frederick Barrett said to Alexander and the other men rowing in Boat 13, "A new moon, turn your money over boys. That is if you have any."

In fact the men had little more than what they were dressed in. The moment that the *Titanic* had slipped beneath the surface the obligation of the White Star Line towards its men had ceased. They were as Alexander's discharge book shows 'Discharged at sea'. All pay ceased from the moment the great liner sank. It is no wonder the men in Boat One accepted Sir Cosmo Duff Gordon's offer of £5 to buy new kit. White Star were not exceptional in the treatment of their men. Other shipping lines operated the same system. This was the second time Alexander had found himself discharged without completing a voyage, the first being when the *Olympic* collided with the cruiser H.M.S. *Hawke* and had to return to Southampton.

At dawn the men on upturned Boat 'B' saw a group of four boats tied together. Blowing a whistle he found in his pocket, Second Officer Lightoller attracted the attention of those in the boats, which resulted in Boats 12 and Four detaching themselves from the others and coming to the aid of those still clinging to Boat 'B'.

John George Phillips,
senior wireless operator

6. THE *CARPATHIA* - SERVICE AS USUAL

Alexander on the Carpathia *still*

wearing his stewards jacket

At 4.10pm the first boat, Boat Two, reached the *Carpathia*. The second lifeboat to reach the *Carpathia* was Boat One, with Sir Cosmo Duff Gordon among its twelve occupants.

As Alexander's boat neared the *Carpathia*, everyone in the boat sang a verse of *Pull for the Shore, Sailor* and then they all cheered. Alexander noted that the weather was bitterly cold and some of the women in his boat were in a very weak state when they finally reached the *Carpathia* at 4.45am. Lawrence Beesley and Dr. Washington Dodge climbed a rope ladder to safety while small children were hauled up in mail sacks. Each new arrival on board was greeted with hot coffee, brandy or tea. Bruce Ismay arrived in Collapsible Boat 'C' at 6.30am. and went straight to the ship's doctor's cabin and remained there. Young Washington Dodge Jr. thought it would be a great joke to hide from his father and not tell his mother that he had seen him. Eventually Steward Ray reunited the family. Also reunited were Ruth Becker with her mother, brother and sister. Only one of the honeymoon couples that had set out from Southampton were still together.

At 8.30am the last boat, Boat 12, arrived at the *Carpathia*. The sea had begun to get rough as Officer Lightoller carefully brought the heavily laden boat alongside. As it now contained those who had spent the night on the upturned Collapsible Boat 'B', the gunwales were almost level with the waves. Harold Bride's feet were frozen and he had to be lifted out of the boat.

By now the *Californian* was standing by having been made aware of the drama which had occurred at dawn. The *Olympic* sent a message to Captain Rostron of the *Carpathia* enquiring if he wanted to transfer his 705 new 'passengers' to the *Titanic's* sister ship. Captain Rostron thought the survivors had suffered enough trauma, without another mid-ocean transfer, so after checking with Bruce Ismay, the offer was declined. At 8.50am Captain Rostron decided there was no more he could do and headed for New York. Passengers on the *Carpathia* gave up their cabins for the survivors and emergency beds were put wherever possible.

Alexander stated that "all our stewards who were rescued by the *Carpathia* set to work looking after the passengers as though on our own ship". Despite the fact that they were doing this work for no pay, the First Class stewards continued to serve 'their' (First Class) passengers, rather than act as survivors of the greatest ever sea tragedy, so strong was the bond between the two groups. It probably crossed Alexander's mind that he might serve some of these people on a future Atlantic crossing. He was equally diplomatic when asked about the treatment of Bruce Ismay when he reached New York. When asked he

Captain Arthur Rostron
of the Carpathia *(seated centre)*
poses with his senior officers.

replied that he thought Mr. Ismay had been treated very harshly by the New York people.

"Mr. Ismay, when he went aboard the *Carpathia*, was taken straight to the doctor's cabin, and there he stopped until he reached New York. The doctor's steward told me he would not eat anything, and that he had only a few biscuits and some water on the way to New York. I think he acted bravely, the way any other Englishman would have done; he was practically pushed into the boat."

This reaction is not surprising when questioned about the chairman of the company which employed him. He was unlikely to say anything detrimental about Ismay if he wanted to remain in employment of the White Star Line.

He was equally generous in his praise for the Engineers when questioned by a reporter. He said he thought the Engineers displayed great bravery in stopping at their posts. There was not a single Engineer saved. In fact, there was that same characteristic of British bravery among all hands. "All the men in our department stood at the boats, and not one of us moved until ordered into the boats."

Alexander's comments of how the British behaved, compared to Italians and other 'foreigners', was very typical of attitudes at the time. Even Third Class passengers were looked down upon. Southampton's postmaster referred to White Star Third Class passengers as 'mostly low class continentals'. Stowaways were referred to as 'Chinese or Japanese' and those who jumped from the decks as 'Italians'. The attitude of the women in Boat 13 to Mr. Foo, showed that they initially viewed him of inferior race to the husbands they had left on the ship and thought of putting him overboard. At the American Inquiry into the disaster, Fifth Officer Lowe had to apologise when he used the term 'acted like an Italian' to infer the man was a coward.

The journey to New York on the *Carpathia* was made worse by a storm that started on the Tuesday evening, 16th April. The storm continued throughout Wednesday and into Thursday morning. Thunder and lightning greeted the *Carpathia* as she reached New York, going first to the White Star Line pier, where the 13 lifeboats she had taken on board were off-loaded. At 9.00pm on Thursday 18th April, she went to Cunard Pier 54 to disembark her passengers.

Some of the First Class survivors, concerned about their status in society, did not wish their arrival on the *Carpathia* to be made public. Reporters were only interested in news of the rich and famous and no mention was made of the other classes or the crew, except for the fate of Captain Smith. While the rich were taken to hotels and special trains which had been laid on for them, the Steerage passengers were cared for by the immigration care societies. Most of these people possessed no more than the clothes they wore.

The crew survivors were no better off as their pay had stopped from the moment the *Titanic* went down. On arrival in New York, crew members were first transferred to the Red Star liner *Lapland* and then put up in a hotel. Every crew survivor was given a complete outfit of clothes (new suit, etc.). Collections were held for them throughout New York and Lookout Frederick Fleet remembered survivors being put behind the counters of a new *Woolworth's* store and told to keep the takings.

Not wanting any more bad publicity, the White Star Line, wanted the crew back as soon as possible on one of their own ships. They attempted to delay the sailing of the *Cedric* which was due to sail for England on the 19th April, but when this was vetoed Alexander sailed for Plymouth on the 20th April aboard the *Lapland*, together with 172 other crew. Thirty-eight other members of crew had to remain in New York to give evidence at the American inquiry into the disaster. After an uneventful crossing the

Lapland arrived in Plymouth Harbour at 7.00am on Monday 29th April. Once ashore they were confined to a waiting room away from the Press who were eager for stories. The waiting room was their accommodation for the night and food and bedding brought in to make them as comfortable as possible. During their detention each crew member was asked to pledge their word of honour that they would issue no statement for publication. It was not until the afternoon of Tuesday 30th April that Alexander and 85 other stewards and stewardesses, finally boarded a train for Southampton. Many of those meeting the train, when it arrived in Southampton at 9.00pm, still had no news of the fate of their relatives and friends in the crew.

Alexander was not required to give evidence at the British Enquiry so he returned to Park House, Hammond Street, Cheshunt, Hertfordshire, where he was re-united with his daughter Winifred.

There he gave the following account to the local paper.

Thirteen of the Titanic's *lifeboats were bought back to New York by the* Carpathia.

7. ALEXANDER LITTLEJOHN'S ACCOUNT

"I was first saloon steward on the *Titanic* and I went off watch about 11 o'clock on Sunday night the 14th April. I went down to my room and sat there with two or three friends. About 11.30pm I went to bed. I had been there some 10 minutes when I was roused by a shaking sort of noise. The whole ship seemed to shake; it was a similar shock to when the *Olympic* dropped a propeller blade. A few seconds afterwards I heard someone shouting "Watertight Door". I got up and dressed and heard someone say that the *Titanic* had hit an iceberg. I went up on the forward part of the ship and on to the top deck. There was about two feet of ice lying in the 'scuppers' on the starboard side. It was very bright overhead and there was a tremendous number of stars, but there was also a slight mist on the water. I did not stay on the top deck for long as I did not regard things as serious. I went one deck down and saw the carpenters sounding the forward well and I noticed there was a quantity of water in it as the line was pulled up. I went back to my room and told the chaps I thought perhaps we might be called on very shortly to assist the passengers, but we did not expect to leave the ship. We all thought she was unsinkable.

We saw a lot of steerage passengers coming from the forward steerage with their lifebelts and carrying their baggage about. We all laughed at these fellows at first and thought they were unnecessarily scared, but when we saw some of them were wet through we knew there must be a lot of water in their quarters. Just then a night watchman came and said; "All hands in the saloon!" That was the first order and while we were getting ready the second steward came down and said: "Every man get on deck at once; put on warm clothing and lifebelts". He added; "Don't leave a man here, or else he will never come out of it perhaps". The remainder of us dressed, put lifebelts on, and went up. We were told to get to the boat stations. In passing along the various decks to my boat station I noticed the bedroom stewards were getting the passengers out and assisting them to get their lifebelts on. I got to my boat, No 11, and helped to get it swung out. I was then told to go down to 'A' deck and assist the women and children into the boat. I went down and assisted in filling the boat with women and children. It was lowered away in charge of the assistant second steward. I went to fill up boat 13, and got about 35 women and children in it. We shouted for more women but there were none forthcoming. We had a few first-class male passengers in. An officer ordered two of us to get in and help row the boat, and I happened to be one of the fortunate ones to be ordered in. The boat was then lowered away, and as we got down to the water we found we were being dropped right

Titanic Survivor's Account

Alexander James Littlejohn

The Weekly Telegraph

(for Waltham Abbey,

Cheshunt & Districts)

printed Friday 10 May 1912.

under the main exhaust pipe. Had we got under that we should have been swamped immediately, but we managed to push the boat on with the oars, although No 15 boat was nearly on top of us.

"The men who did the lowering of the boats", proceeded Mr. Littlejohn, "are worthy of the greatest praise for the admirable manner in which they worked. We pulled away from the ship into safety. We then 'lay on our oars' and watched. We could see the Titanic gradually sinking by the head. Her forward 'E' deck ports were under the water, and we could see the lights gradually go out on the 'E' deck as she settled down. All her other lights were burning brilliantly and she looked a blaze of light from stem to stern. We watched her like this for some time, and then suddenly she gave a plunge forward and all the lights went out. Her stern went right up in the air; there were two or three explosions and it appeared to me the stern part came down again and righted itself. Immediately after there were terrible cries for help. They were awful and heartrending.

Soon after this we sighted a light which we thought was a steamer and which I still believe was one. We pulled towards it but we did not appear to get any nearer to it, and after a time the light disappeared. We pulled about during the night and kept in touch with other boats, until just before dawn the lights of the *Carpathia* were sighted. We waited for daylight to come and as soon as it was light we rowed towards her. We found we were practically surrounded by ice; one iceberg as large as the Isle of Wight lay close by us. The weather was bitterly cold and some of the women in our boat were in a very weak state when we reached the *Carpathia*. We were picked up by the *Carpathia* and proceeded to New York. All our stewards who were saved by the *Carpathia* set to work looking after the passengers as though on our own ship." "Did you see any thing of the captain?" queried the writer.

"I saw him", answered Mr. Littlejohn, "near his cabin when I went to the boat deck. I think he was speaking to the chief officer at the time".

"Can you account for the rumour that the captain shot himself?" "There is no truth in that. I know other fellows who saw him much later than I did, and he was not the sort of man to shoot himself.

There was a great friend of mine - a steward named Brown - was saved after being in the water some hours. He told me he was washed off the bridge as the forward funnel dipped and that the captain was on the bridge at the time and said to the other stewards around him, "Do what you can for yourselves boys."

"Was there any actual shooting?" - "The chief officer I think it was, shot one of the Italian waiters belonging to the restaurant because he got into a boat and would not come out of it when he was told to. I think another officer fired his revolver to frighten some foreigners who were looking over the side and intended to jump into a boat as it was being lowered."

Alexander, October 1912
his hair having turned white.

964.T.
THE ILL-FATED WHITE STAR LINER "TITANIC." THE LARGEST SHIP IN THE WORLD, WHICH FOUNDERED
WITH A LOSS OF 1503 LIVES. 15th OF APRIL 1912, OFF NEWFOUNDLAND ON HER MAIDEN VOYAGE.

Titanic postcard,
issued after the sinking.

In memorium card
(front and reverse) 1912.
Collection of Anne Sorensen

"Did you hear the band playing the hymn *Nearer my God to Thee*?" "The band were playing when we left the ship. At the time she went under we were nearly half a mile off. The band might have been playing that hymn, but I did not hear it. What I could hear was the awful cries from the people. The sounds are ringing in my ears now."

In reply to another query, Mr. Littlejohn said he thought that Mr. Bruce Ismay had been very harshly treated by the New York people. "Mr. Ismay, when he went aboard the *Carpathia*, was taken straight to the doctor's cabin, and there he stopped until he reached New York. The doctor's steward told me he would not eat anything, and that he had only a few biscuits and some water on the way to New York. I think he acted bravely, the way any other Englishman would have done; he was practically pushed into the boat."

Asked if he saw anything of Mr. Stead, Mr. Littlejohn said he last saw him in the reception room at night, just after dinner. He handed him a large cup of coffee, and that was the last time he saw him.

Mr. Littlejohn concluded the interview by stating that he thought the engineers displayed great bravery in stopping at their posts. There was not a single engineer saved. In fact, there was that same characteristic of British bravery among all hands. "All the men in our department stood at the boats, and not one of us moved until ordered into the boats."

Embroidered bookmark featuring Nearer my God to Thee, *thought by some to be the last tune played by the* Titanic's *orchestra.*

8. AFTER THE *TITANIC*

Alexander returned to sea on the 23rd October 1912, when he sailed on the White Star liner the *Oceanic* from Southampton, bound for New York. The *Oceanic* was also captained by a Captain Smith, but this time it was Captain Harry Smith who was in command. Alexander received a new *Continuous Certificate of Discharge Book* to replace the one lost on the *Titanic*. This clearly showed the effect the sinking had made on him. His hair which six months before had been dark was now recorded as white. He had removed his moustache as all his facial hair including his eyebrows had gone white. His date of birth appeared in this book as 1876 when his birth certificate shows clearly he was born in 1872. Was this a mistake or was Alexander deducting a few years to compensate for his white-haired appearance?

In all, Alexander made six voyages on the *Oceanic*, the fifth under the captaincy of Captain Herbert J. Haddock. He had been in command of the *Olympic* when she received the distress signals from the *Titanic* on the 15th April.

The *Olympic* became strike-bound at the end of April 1912, when many of her crew left the ship and would not return until sufficient lifeboats were fitted. In the winter of 1912/13, *Olympic* returned to Harland and Wolff in Belfast for an extensive refit. The double bottom with which both the *Olympic* and the *Titanic* had been fitted was extended up the sides of the *Olympic* to form a double skin. The bulkheads between the watertight compartments were made higher and more life saving equipment was installed.

Alexander rejoined the *Olympic* on the 4th June 1913 where he met up with Steward Sidney Daniels with whom he had sailed on both the maiden voyage of the *Olympic* and the *Titanic*. Sidney Daniels was only aged only 18 when he sailed on the *Titanic*. He survived the sinking by swimming to the upturned Collapsible Boat 'B' and sitting on the keel until rescue came.

The Lapland *on which Alexander returned to England after the sinking.*

I was fortunate enough to meet Sidney Daniels and his wife in Portsmouth, before he died in 1983. He still had his locker keys from the *Titanic,* which were in his pocket when he left the ship. A remarkable man, he escaped death a second time while serving in the trenches in World War I, after a shell landed, embedding itself in his thigh, but failing to explode.

The voyage to New York on the 4th June 1913 under the captaincy of Captain Haddock was to be the first of 21 consecutive voyages Alexander made on the *Olympic* with the same captain. The sequence was to come to an end on the 28th October 1914 when the *Olympic* returned to Glasgow, having left there on the 9th October to sail to New York.

The outbreak of World War I, in August 1914, had meant that the *Olympic's* schedules had to be rearranged with the voyage which had started from Southampton on the 29th July, returning back to Liverpool on the 16th August 1914. The following two voyages for the *Olympic* to New York both started and ended in Liverpool. Before she was taken out of commercial service at the end of October 1914, the *Olympic* rescued the crew of a British battleship which had struck a mine off the coast of Ireland.

Alexander was finally discharged on the 3rd November 1914 in Belfast, where he had originally joined the *Titanic* in March 1912, his life at sea finally over. Forty-two-years old and in failing health he was prevented from taking any further part in active service in World War I.

On his retirement from the sea Alexander first went to live with his brother Clement and sister Emily, who were both unmarried and shared a house at 93, Carlyle Road, Manor Park, London. Clement worked as a booking office clerk at Fenchurch Street Station, and Emily, as a matron at the Mile End Workhouse.

Alexander took an office job becoming a Relief Officer. In March 1923 he married his second wife Mary Elizabeth Tyler and moved to 253, Romford Road, Forest Gate, Essex. Mrs. Tyler at the age of 39 years was 10 years his junior. The wedding certificate shows her as a widow, but research in Australia, from where Mrs. Tyler originated showed that at the time of the marriage Mr. Tyler, a travelling musician, was still very much alive and on his travels in Australia! Alexander I'm sure was unaware of this. To add to the complications his son, Alexander Francis, married Mrs. Tyler's daughter, Florence.

While being entirely legal, this meant that my uncle's wife was also his step-sister. Her mother, his step-mother, was also his mother-in-law!

Allowance & holiday grant,
sent three weeks before
Alexander died.

*Alexander with his
grand-daughter Anne 1940*

*Alexander & his son
Alexander Francis c1918*

*Alexander at the
Christening of his
grandson, Alexander
Sorensen. At that time
he was registered as
blind. 1940*

*Clement, Emily &
Alexander c1930*

*Alexander
(third from left)
at the author's
Christening 1943*

Alexander and his second wife moved their final address 27, Ethelbert Gardens, Ilford, Essex in 1930. He had now retired and my mother remembers him, at her wedding to Harry, as looking very frail and being registered as blind. He continued to receive a grant from time to time from the National Disasters Relief Fund for survivors of the *Titanic* and the *Lusitania*. After an operation for the removal of a cataract he did partially regain his sight.

His second wife died in January 1948, leaving the house which she owned to her daughter and her grandsons. Alexander could remain living there for the rest of his life. On the 31st August 1949, he received his final grant for a holiday, but before he was able to take that holiday, he died, on the 18th September 1949. He was buried beside his first wife Anne in Cheshunt Cemetery.

I am often asked if I have any memory of my grandfather, but as I was only six years old when he died, I do not. My father, who died some years ago, said that the subject of the *Titanic* was not something his father mentioned, although he himself was interested in the story. It is my father I have to thank for keeping all the memorabilia I have connected with the *Titanic* and the *Olympic*.

My mother remembers Alexander as being always smartly dressed with his white pocket handkerchief. She found him and his family quite difficult, and Emily opposed her marriage to Henry (or anybody else). Emily finally married in 1941, at the age of 72. Alexander's brother Clement never married.

His daughter, Winifred May married a Dane, Christian Sorenson and together they established a nursery growing tomatoes in Nazeing, Essex. Their daughter, Anne, (named after Alexander's wife) wears a ring in which is mounted a half sovereign. This was given to her mother by Alexander, who had it in his pocket when he was ordered into Boat 13 - a tip from a passenger in the First Class Saloon? We shall never know but a coin certainly that travelled on the *Titanic*.

There is now no Alexander Littlejohn in any branch of our family, but hopefully the memory of Alexander James Littlejohn, for whom the number 13, brought not only tragedy, but also his means of survival on the *Titanic*, will live on for years to come.

Alexander c1918

Alexander & his second wife
Mary Elizabeth Tyler c1930

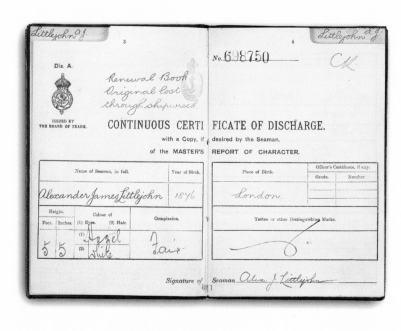

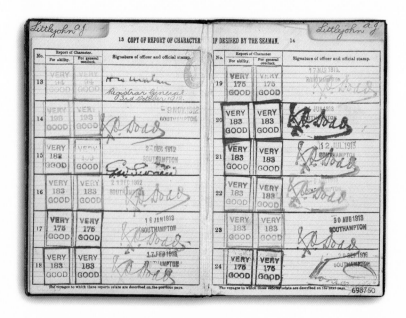

A selection of pages from Alexander's Continuous Certificate of Discharge book. This was re-issued on his return to duty after the disaster and records the Titanic *as his 13th voyage .*

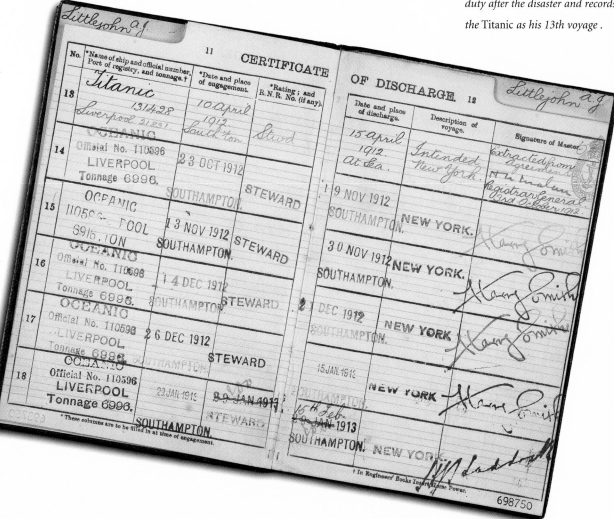

9. ON REFLECTION

I was once asked the question by my daughter "How did grandfather survive when so many people died?"

I believe the honest answer to that question is; "he was very lucky." He was probably known to Sixth Officer Moody who was in charge of loading boat 13 as they had sailed together on the *Olympic*. When it came to choosing men to row the boat, Moody would have gone for someone known to him, even though he had no idea of the man's ability as an oarsman. The inclusion of stewards in the boats was to provide care for the passengers.

Alexander was also very fortunate that his boat was on the starboard side, rather than on the port side, where Officer Lightoller strictly enforced the 'women and children only' rule.

During his time as a landlord in Hastings, Alexander, was a prominent mason and sent his son to the Royal Masonic School. I have often wondered if officers and other crew members were aware of his membership of this brotherhood and if this was a factor in his survival.

I find it difficult to understand why a man suffering from rheumatism, which affected his sight, would choose at the age of thirty-nine, to leave three children aged 10, 8, and 3 years, whose mother had just died, and go to sea. Was he heart-broken at the loss of Anne, or was it cash he needed to support his family? He had no house, having been a landlord, but he had family and friends, who were willing to care for his children. Or did he prefer the single life, like his brother Clement and his sister Emily, free to travel wherever he pleased?

The other unanswerable question is; what effect did the death of W. T. Stead have on world history? Stead was such a powerful figure; on his way to America, to address a meeting on world peace alongside President Taft of the U.S.A., when he lost his life on the *Titanic*. He talked with world leaders, such as the Tsar of Russia, and through journalism sought to influence and promote the cause of world peace. When the German Kaiser boasted to him in 1910, about the fast growing German navy, Stead passed on this information to the then First Sea Lord, 'Jackie' Fisher. He also promoted the cause of women's rights and supported the suffragette movement. Had he lived, and continued working for these causes, one wonders what effect this would have had on the forces that came together, to bring the world to war in 1914.

W. T. Stead was a strong swimmer and said that he would never drown. He was also very interested in the world of spiritualism and communicating with 'the other side'. I was told the following story by Stead's biographer, Victor Pierce Jones, who lives very close to Stead's home on Hayling Island, Holly Bush House.

The owner of Holly Bush House in 1975, Mrs Jean Cambridge, went into one of the upstairs bedrooms and discovered a large wet patch on the carpet. Nothing had been spilt , there were no leaks, and the room felt very cold. There was nothing to explain where the water had come from....................................It was just as if a wet, dripping, figure had stood at that spot for some time.

At the time of writing this book Holly Bush House was for sale and was attracting a lot of interest from *Titanic* enthusiasts around the world. The spirit of W. T. Stead lives on!

LUCKY 13?

1. The 13th voyage shown in Alexander's
   Continuous Certificate of Discharge book was the *Titanic*.

2. Alexander was rescued in Boat 13.

3. Boat 13 - the 13th boat launched.

4. 13 lifeboats taken to New York by the *Carpathia*.

5. 13 people picked up from the sea by lifeboat.

   • Boat 'D' - One person

   • Boat 14 - Four people

   this was the boat which returned under the command of Fifth Officer Lowe.

   • Boat Four - Eight people

   this boat was still close to the *Titanic* when she went down.

6. Morgan Robertson in his 1898 story *Futility*
   wrote that 13 people survived the sinking of the *Titan*.

7. On the 13th April, W. T. Stead dreams of
   "someone throwing cats off a tall building". This was the night before the tragedy.

FACTS ABOUT THE *TITANIC*

LENGTH. 882FT 9INS

BEAM OR WIDTH. 92FT 6INS

HULL DEPTH 59FT 6INS

HEIGHT (Keel to Bridge). 104FT

(To Top of Funnels) 175FT

TONNAGE . . . . 46,328 TONS

DISPLACEMENT . . . . 60,000 TONS

DECKS 10

BOILERS (24 Double Ended, 5 Single Ended - in 6 rooms) 29

FURNACES. 159

FUNNELS (No 1, 2, 3, for Boiler Smoke, No 4 for Ventilation) 4

ANCHORS (3 at the Bow, Centre 15 1/2 Tons, Sides 7 1/2 Tons). 3

WATERTIGHT COMPARTMENTS. 16

BULKHEADS

(First Two & last Five up to "D' Deck middle Eight up to "E' Deck) 15

ENGINES (2 Four Cylinder Reciprocating Engines -1 Turbine

Driving Centre Propellor Recycling Steam from the Main Engines) . . . 3

PROPELLERS (Left & Right-3 Blades, Centre-4 Blades). 3

TOTAL HORSEPOWER. 46,000

SERVICE SPEED. . . . . 21 KNOTS

TOP SPEED. . . . . 24-25 KNOTS

MAXIMUM PASSENGERS AND CREW 3,547

NUMBER OF LIFEBOATS (16 + 4 Collapsibles - 1,176 Places). 20

GLOSSARY OF TERMS

AFT	Towards the stern of a ship
AMIDSHIPS	The middle of the ship
BOW (OR HEAD)	Front part of the ship
BRIDGE	Raised platform from which the ship is steered.
BULKHEAD	Upright partition dividing ship into compartments
CQD	Distress code used before SOS
COLLAPSIBLE BOATS	
(A, B, C and D)	wooden bottomed lifeboats with canvas sides (The sides were collapsed when stored and raised when in use)
CROW'S NEST	Barrel on mast for use of lookouts.
DAVITS	Small cranes used for lowering lifeboats.
FORWARD	Towards the bow
GALLEYS	Ships kitchens
GLORY HOLE	Stewards, crew living quarters
GROWLERS	Small, low, flat icebergs
HMS	His (or Her) Majesty's Ship - used by the Royal Navy.
KNOT	Unit of speed equivalent to one nautical mile per hour (one nautical mile equals 6,080 feet)
"LAY ON OUR OARS"	Stopped rowing
MUSTER	To assemble the ship's crew
PORT	The left-hand side of the ship looking forward
RMS	Royal Mail Steamer. Both *Olympic* and *Titanic* prefixed by these letters.
SCUPPERS	The edge of the deck where water (or ice) collected.
SOS	Distress signal ... --- ... in Morse Code.
SOUNDING THE WELL	Checking for water inside the ship.
STARBOARD	The right-hand side of the ship looking forward.
STEERAGE	Passenger occupying the cheapest accommodation. (Third Class passengers on the *Olympic* and *Titanic*)
STERN	Rear end of the ship
STOKER	Crewman who works at the ship's furnaces.
TRIMMER	Crewman who delivers coal to the stokers on a ship.
WATERTIGHT DOORS	Steel doors that could be closed in an emergency to seal off a compartment and make it watertight

BIBLIOGRAPHY

WALTER LORD	*A Night to Remember* - Penguin	1976
DON LYNCH & KEN MARSCHALL	*Titanic-An Illustrated History* Hodder & Stoughton / Madison Press	1992
JOHN P EATON & CHARLES A HAAS	*Titanic -Triumph and Tragedy* Patrick Stephens	1986
DONALD HYSLOP, ALISTAIR FORSYTH, SHEILA JEMINA	*Titanic Voices - Memories from the Fateful Voyage* Sutton Publishing/St Martins Press, New York.	1994
TOM McCLUSKIE	*Anatomy of the Titanic* - PRC Publishing	1998
GEOFF TIBBALLS	*The Titanic* - Carlton Books	1997
Dr. ROBERT BALLARD	*The Discovery of the Titanic* Hodder & Stoughton / Maddison Press	1987
VICTOR PIERCE JONES	*Saint or Sensationalist?* The story of W. T. Stead Gooday Publishers	1988
LAWRENCE BEESLEY	*The Loss of the Titanic* - Heinemann	1912
COLONEL ARCHIBALD GRACIE	*Titanic - A Survivor's Story* Allan Sutton Publishing	1985
DAISY CORNING STONE SPEDDING	*Polar - The Titanic Bear* Madison Press	1994
PHILIP GIBBS	*The Deathless Story of the Titanic* Peter Way Ltd.	1972

ACKNOWLEDGEMENTS

To my wife Jean and my daughter Hannah for all their help and support.
Brian Ticehurst for his expert comments
John Fry (BTS) for his advice
My cousin, Anne Sorensen
Jason Horsburgh
Michael Wicks
and everyone who has made a contribution to this book.

Photograph and Illustration Credits
Every effort has been made to correctly attribute all material reproduced in this book. If any errors have unwittingly occurred, I will be happy to correct them in future editions.

1-8	- All author's collection
9,10	- 17 BPL
11	- Hulton-Getty
12,13	- Author's collection
17	- Ken Marschall Collection
18	- Walter Lord Collection
21	- John P Eaton and Charles A Haas
23	- The Cork Examiner
24	- Illustrated London News
33	- ILN
34	- Daily Mirror
35	- Daily Sketch
37	- (top) Mr & Mrs Arthur Dodge
37	- (bottom) Private collection
39	- Illustrated London News
44	- Mr & Mrs George A Fenwick
45	- Paul Louden-Brown/Courtesy of Ocean Liner Society
47	- Brown Brothers
48-57	- Author's collection
50	- Anne Sorensen
52	- Daily Sketch
54	- Anne Sorensen